Paul Skinner is the founder of the Agency of the Future, which helps clients drive purpose-led change and better mobilise stakeholders for lasting success. He advises global businesses and pioneering charities and social enterprises as well as institutions of international and global governance.

He is also the founder of MarketingKind, a membership community which brings together business leaders, marketers and change-makers to tackle social and environmental problems through their businesses, volunteering and advocacy.

T0244055

Praise for *The Purpose Upgrade*

'*The Purpose Upgrade* is thoughtful, practical and inspiring. The private sector can and must play a key role in overcoming the significant challenges the world is facing. After all, as a business you cannot be successful – nor call yourself successful – in a society that fails. Impact and leadership come with responsibility, and this book offers must-have insights for leaders from across all industries'

Feike Sijbesma, CEO of Royal DSM (2007–2020), Co-Chair Global Climate Adaptation Centers, Fortune World's 50 Greatest Leaders (2018) and UN Humanitarian of the Year 2010

'In today's world, every business needs to put purpose above profit. Paul's book is a necessary and enlightening call to action for businesses to re-think why they exist and the implications for everything they say, think and do'

Mike Berners-Lee, author of *There Is No Planet B*

'*The Purpose Upgrade* is an important book that feeds the imagination. Most importantly it is a book about emotional intelligence and the energy unlocked by doing the right thing. Never underestimate the power of feeling good about yourself and the people around you. Read this book and become something greater than you previously thought possible'

Sir Tim Smit KBE, Co-Founder of the Eden Project

'This brilliantly original work weaves a fascinating range of cutting-edge ideas into a cogent argument for fundamentally rethinking how organisations understand and pursue their core purpose. As the world faces up to its radically uncertain future, Paul Skinner's highly engaging text challenges us all to create a "Wealth of Change". It is a book full of humanity and hope'

Gareth Owen OBE, Humanitarian Director of Save the Children

'Paul Skinner is one of the best and here he tackles the purpose agenda with erudition and originality. His book will be standard reading for everyone who seeks a Purpose Upgrade personally or professionally'

Sue Unerman, Chief Transformation Officer of MediaCom and co-author of *Belonging*

'Paul Skinner has written a most engaging and readable book, both visionary and practical. It builds on his earlier thesis of Collaborative Advantage by challenging organisational leaders to coalesce stakeholders' energies towards higher societal or even global goals. I have personally seen how his ideas have been remarkably effective in the efforts of International Civil Society organisations. The scale of our crises now means we need businesses capable of addressing our greatest challenges and I urge leaders everywhere to answer this timely call to action and follow this greater path to success'

Sir Brendan Gormley KCMG, former Chief Executive of the Disasters and Emergencies Committee

'In some ways the tragedy of recent capitalism is that, while it has ostensibly created a breadth of wealth and opportunity, it has narrowed the minds of everyone who participates in it. The shareholder value movement was a great example of this. This book is a necessary and timely contribution to a more organic, more nuanced and more complete appreciation of what a business can achieve'

Rory Sutherland, Vice-Chair of Ogilvy and the *Spectator*'s 'Wikiman'

'Paul Skinner's latest book, *The Purpose Upgrade*, has to be an essential read for everyone in business, whether an entrepreneur, CEO or marketing chief – or in fact anyone who cares about the future of humankind. Paul has not only led the way in conscious marketing in the UK as well as globally, but is one of the most intelligent people I know and his perspective on how to combine purpose, business, the future of society and indeed the world is absolutely crucial understanding for us all'

Lynne Franks OBE, social entrepreneur, author and Founder of the SEED Women's Leadership Platform

'As we face into what some might argue is the greatest reset of the modern era, *The Purpose Upgrade* challenges us to think deeply about what purpose really means, while providing us with a framework for bringing true meaning and purpose to organisational culture, aligning corporate aspiration with stakeholder ambition. A must-read for anyone who cares about the role they, and their organisation, play in creating a whole that is much more meaningful than its constituent parts'

Célia Pronto, Managing Director of Love Home Swap and Non-Executive Director of South East Water, Moto Hospitality and Samworth Brothers

'This moment of global jeopardy is not one for business to abandon or push back on social and environmental purpose; rather, the reverse. Paul Skinner's timely book makes the case for "re-purposing" enterprise – and, importantly, sets out how this can be done'

Simon Maxwell CBE, former Director of the Overseas Development Institute

'This excellent book will change how you think about the purpose of your organisation. A tangible manifesto for organisations to build greater value with all stakeholders, to become stronger and more sustainable'

Peter Seymour, Vice-President of Marketing and Strategy Europe at Mondelēz

'If purpose was "nice to have" in plain-sailing business conditions, it's vital in the stormy waters we now find ourselves navigating. Paul's timely and richly evidenced book shows how a well-defined purpose can magnetise and revitalise your organisation. Required reading for pathfinding leaders, change agents and entrepreneurs'

John Grant, author of *Greener Marketing*

'*The Purpose Upgrade* offers a profoundly human response to the challenges facing businesses today. It provides the insight, wisdom and practicality required for leaders to succeed by creating the more inclusive and sustainable future we so urgently need'

Sophie Devonshire, Chief Executive of The Marketing Society and co-author of *Love Work*

'As a policy researcher and analyst, I often say that the biggest contribution an individual can make to changing the world is advocating for the policy they believe in. Paul Skinner has convinced me of another truth: "If you want to change the world, there may be no greater lever to pull than to find a solution to a problem and to deliver and scale that solution through meaningful enterprise." Skinner explains the origin of purpose, then offers fascinating examples of how purposeful enterprises and organisations tackle societal problems. Finally, he raises questions and offers advice for those attempting a Purpose Upgrade. There's a lot of wisdom packed into this book's pages!'

Joan Fitzgerald, Professor of Urban Planning and Public Affairs at Northeastern University and author of *Greenovation*

'Reading *The Purpose Upgrade* encourages us to view purpose through an interconnected lens, compelling and challenging us to rethink everything that's been alluded to as "purpose": re-imagining the problems you seek to solve, re-designing the solutions you offer and uplifting the goals you seek to achieve in the first place. Important and urgent. Read it. Absorb. Ponder. Question. Upgrade your purpose'

Michelle Carvill, entrepreneur and co-author of *Sustainable Marketing*

'*The Purpose Upgrade* is a reflection of Paul's business experience at the Agency of the Future and MarketingKind, along with practical case studies, exploring how we can transform not only the way in which we do business but our business itself – the "why" then the "what" of the enterprise. It is an invitation to a deeper reflection on the kind of economic system we should decide to build together'

Daniela Barone Soares, Chief Executive of Snowball Impact Investments and Non-Executive Director of Intercontinental Hotels Group and Halma PLC

'*The Purpose Upgrade* takes you along a series of "stops" in which you'll explore all aspects of purpose, from the theory through to the planning and the all-important practical application. Purpose is a word that has become overused and misunderstood, which in turn has meant it has somewhat lost its super-power. This book overcomes the limitations of prior approaches and re-defines the core role purpose can play in helping us achieve a greater success by taking on the most pressing societal and environmental challenges we face. *The Purpose Upgrade* will help us lead the way in striving for a more sustainable future for people and planet'

Gemma Butler, co-author of *Sustainable Marketing*

'It would be almost impossible to read this book and not feel inspired and driven to throw yourself straight into the valuable work of upgrading the purpose of your enterprise, changing lives for the better and building a stronger commercial business, with greater engagement from all stakeholders in so doing. *The Purpose Upgrade* provides a complete methodology to re-define and embed your purpose, facing into the realities of the challenge, in driving and embedding change'

Abigail Dixon, author of *The Whole Marketer* and Founder of Labyrinth Marketing

'Every great book always contains a single sentence that anchors its richness and this one is no exception: "True listening best begins by taking an interest in the lives and priorities of the people we serve in their own terms". That's what purpose ultimately is: listening, planning and acting together with people and planet, not on our terms but on theirs, and here's a route map to turn this higher truth into granular action across all you do'

Mike Barry, former Head of Sustainable Business at M&S

Also by Paul Skinner

*Collaborative Advantage: How collaboration beats
competition as a strategy for success*

Praise for *Collaborative Advantage*

'Critics of communism often remark that the system, though wonderful in theory, was fatally incompatible with human nature. But the same criticism could be levelled perfectly well at the many current assumptions of modern capitalism. What makes us human is not that we compete – anything can do that: as this book explains, our real difference lies in our near-miraculous powers of collaboration. *Collaborative Advantage* offers the perfect recipe for successful businesses that improve lives'

**Ben Cohen and Jerry Greenfield,
Co-Founders of Ben and Jerry's**

'This is a profound provocation as to the imperative of a collaborative mindset in an ever-more volatile world. Paul has defined a model and brought it to life with a wide variety of helpful examples, making it applicable to almost any challenge a business or brand might face.'

**Mark Evans, Managing Director of
Marketing & Digital at Direct Line Group**

'Truly paradigm-shifting books are rare, but Paul's argument seems to me both revolutionary and inevitable.'

**Alison Jones, coach, strategist and host of
The Extraordinary Business Book Club and
author of *This Book Means Business***

'The new business formula in a world of open innovation and creativity is about getting on and not just getting ahead. Co-operation is no longer a niche. It is a core competence. This book by Paul Skinner, the great advocate of Collaborative Advantage, is a handbook for success in this new commercial world'

**Ed Mayo, Chief Executive of Pilotlight and
former Secretary General of Co-operatives UK**

CHANGE YOUR BUSINESS
TO SAVE THE WORLD

THE PURPOSE UPGRADE

CHANGE THE WORLD TO
SAVE YOUR BUSINESS

Paul Skinner

ROBINSON

ROBINSON

First published in Great Britain in 2022 by Robinson

1 3 5 7 9 10 8 6 4 2

ISBN: 978-1-47214-518-5

Typeset in Perpetua by Hewer Text UK Ltd, Edinburgh
Printed and bound in Great Britain by Clays Ltd, Elcograf S.p.A

Robinson
An imprint of
Little, Brown Book Group
Carmelite House
50 Victoria Embankment
London EC4Y 0DZ
An Hachette UK Company

www.hachette.co.uk

www.littlebrown.co.uk

How To Books are published by Robinson, an imprint of Little, Brown Book Group. We welcome
proposals from authors who have first-hand experience of their subjects. Please set out the aims of
your book, its target market and its suggested contents in an email to howto@littlebrown.co.uk

CONTENTS

Preface

GREATER EXPECTATIONS

'What keeps you awake at night?'

I was once asked this question at the start of a panel discussion as part of a study on global risk run by the defence think-tank RUSI and King's College London.

The other panellists had more domain expertise than I did. They included a range of global business leaders from sectors with a particular focus on risk, a senior UN official, a director of the Space Agency and a former government minister who had held responsibility for the UK's resilience for six years.

Various disaster scenarios were discussed, from a cyber-attack that takes out the internet to a collapse of the energy grid to devastating increases in the displacement of peoples. But crises don't threaten us in isolation. The greatest difficulties usually lie in coping with the knock-on effects that they cause. My concerns were therefore less about a specific hazard than about how we can become more capable of adapting to a world of greater disruption.

We are now living through times in which, while anything may seem possible, little appears certain. The pandemic has shown us, in case we didn't know it before, that our own efforts can be futile if our operating environment does not allow us to maintain them. And it is entirely likely that our greatest challenges lie ahead, in the form of a long recovery amid further economic shocks, the increasing threat of conflict and a social, political, technological and environmental context replete with questions for which there are often no clear precedents to guide us.

It would be easy to conclude that our own volition is in vain when we cannot control the major forces that have an impact on the success that we can achieve. And yet there has never been a greater need and opportunity for deliberate action. While we may have allowed many of our biggest problems to arise by accident, we now have to solve them together on purpose.

When Russia invaded Ukraine in February 2022, the Ukrainian response was completely different than in the prior invasion of 2014, in large part because the Ukrainians had learned to be far better prepared the second time around. The ultimate COVID vaccine may now need to come, metaphorically, in the form of learning from our direct exposure to one global crisis the lessons that we need to be able to repurpose and revitalise our businesses, organisations and institutions when confronted with an increased range and frequency of existential challenges. Rebooting, re-setting and even building back better are not enough as they imply a return to a prior normality rooted in a world that no longer exists. What is required is a renewable capacity for purpose-driven change that supports us in tackling our most important problems head on.

Businesses today too often fall short in their capacity to achieve this. For many businesses, the purpose through which they previously achieved their success now blinds them to more important realities. As a consequence, economic activity still accelerates the climate emergency, drives a mass extinction of species, depletes the resources most essential to life, and exacerbates inequalities. It also too often profits from and exploits the amplification of intolerance and untruthfulness. This divides us from each other and curbs our capacity for cooperation, leaving us more, rather than less, exposed to the risks that we face.

Compelling evidence now shows, however, that by playing their part in tackling society's most pressing priorities, enterprises can create more attractive benefits for customers, build more meaningful livelihoods for colleagues, and unlock superior returns for investors, thereby bringing all the stakeholders that a business needs into alignment around a greater ambition. Addressing the increasingly urgent United Nations' Sustainable Development Goals alone is already estimated to be a twelve trillion-dollar opportunity, without taking into account the almost limitless life-supporting opportunities that lie beyond their direct scope. Fulfilling true human need rather than manufacturing spurious consumerist wants has become the biggest business opportunity of our time.

This will often require us to reconsider how we form the purpose of our enterprises and other organisations in the first place. We typically think of purpose as fixed, like a North Star; that it comes from within our organisation and that it is singular. These are just some of the half-truths that have come to hold us back. In *The Purpose Upgrade*, I shall argue that there is no single-end fixed point and that to achieve our greatest success we must instead cultivate a purpose which responds to society's changing needs, is created with and through our external as well as internal stakeholders, and integrates many layers of goals and aspirations in a living wholeness through an evolving nexus of reciprocal benefits.

Can enterprise support us in overcoming the obstacles that we now face? Can business enable us to enjoy a material comfort enhanced through shared experience with others rather than obtained at their expense? And can it help us to adapt to a rapidly shifting environment in which the potential for success may be great but the threats are also very real?

Our problems are also our gateways to the future. The direct experience of the pandemic and subsequent crises, from conflict to the rising cost of living, has created an environment of readiness for change in which we can see that bigger ideas can and must now take hold. The hardest times can also offer the most far-reaching opportunities for renewal. My aim in writing *The Purpose Upgrade* therefore has been to provide the provocation, methodology and support needed to repurpose any enterprise and revitalise the activities within it.

We can address no greater need than to change our businesses to save the world and find no greater opportunity than to change the world to save our businesses.

Ce qui est simple est toujours faux. Ce qui ne l'est pas est inutilisable.
Anything simple is false. And everything that isn't is unusable.

Paul Valéry

Every end in history necessarily contains a new beginning.

Hannah Arendt

THE ENTERPRISE OF HOPE

Dr Mick Jackson had a clear goal to achieve.

He had set out to climb the adjoining mountains K2 and Broad Peak.

A young French boy was then found dead in his tent just ahead of Mick's expedition.

He had been killed by the biting cold and ever thinner atmosphere. The military sent a crew to air-lift his corpse from the mountain in a body-bag strapped to their helicopter. It was the only way to extract him. It would take a week of hiking over ice to reach even the base of these mountains.

Mick and his companions were guided by a Kashmiri tribesman. As conditions became even more challenging, the tribesman too subsequently lost consciousness. A group ascending the mountain just behind them by chance included the Bulgarian Minister for Health. He was still a practising doctor and examined the tribesman, reporting that his lungs had collapsed. He would die within twenty-four hours if left at that altitude. The military refused to send another helicopter. Mick supposed this was because a living tribesman had less money than a dead westerner and was therefore considered less of a priority. The guide bowed his head, folded his arms and accepted his fate.

But Mick was less willing to accept the situation. He gathered together several of the Kashmiri tribesmen and over the course of four days managed the arduous descent to rescue his guide from the mountain. By the end most of the group, including Mick, were coughing blood from the biting conditions. But they all made it.

Those four days were life-saving for the Kashmiri guide. But they were also life-changing for Mick. The only need for the ordeal of the gruelling lift to safety in the face of sub-zero temperatures, he reasoned, was because a man was being judged by the authorities on the basis of his possessions and deemed unworthy of help.

It cut to the heart of Mick's values. As a former professional musician, he valued individual creativity and freedom. But right at the core of his soul, Mick cherished his identity as a descendent from highlanders and Irish immigrants. He felt a deep solidarity with people braving tough conditions. His grandfathers had each worked as miners from the age of twelve and his father had the knife wounds to show for the life that he had lived as an outsider growing up in a Glasgow slum. Mick believed that they too would have been left on the mountain if a similar fate had befallen them.

In a moment that would change the course of his life and career, he promised himself that when he returned home, he would find a way to repurpose his business activities to make a difference. He didn't yet know what he would do, but he had found a reason to take action that would give entirely new meaning to his entrepreneurial activities.

He had no desire to create a charity or set about fundraising, reasoning that he didn't want to divert existing flows of donations. Instead, he sought to build a different relationship between people and enterprise. He wanted to harness the resources of business to empower people, helping them to help themselves and fulfil their own potential so that they would not suffer the indignity of exclusion.

Looking at industry through this new lens, he sought out sectors of activity that few people usually find interesting. He landed on stationery products and other office supplies, because they are universally needed but, as Mick has put it to me, no one cares about who supplies them: 'Paper clips and envelopes rarely make the pages of *Fast Company* magazine or the *Harvard Business Review.*' Taking aim at such a 'boring' sector, he repurposed stationery provision as a service to fund micro-finance initiatives to help some of the world's most excluded people to lift themselves out of poverty.

Mick named his enterprise WildHearts Office, and established its mission to empower people globally through the profits from office supplies. The idea that money spent every day by businesses could be channelled to create positive impact brought a bigger meaning to office supplies than the procurement managers whom Mick talked to had ever previously heard in a sales pitch. It consequently gained rapid traction and grew faster than he could possibly have anticipated. The WildHearts Foundation, which Mick created to distribute the profits from WildHearts Office in the form of micro-loans to the world's poorest, reached more than 1.25 million people with micro-finance in under four years. It now owns the biggest banks for the rural poor in Malawi and Zambia and addresses some of the most challenging needs in Zimbabwe. During the time of writing this book, the number of lives that WildHearts has transformed has passed two million.

Mick's quest has not followed the kind of linear path that could have been anticipated from the outset. Fresh opportunities have revealed themselves progressively as he has built his social enterprise, with each new peak revealing a fresh height to climb behind it. When he learned that the majority of the world's women are excluded from finance altogether, for example, he prioritised women in WildHearts' micro-finance programmes, empowering them to feed their children, enabling their daughters to attend school, and ultimately giving them a voice that has counted often for the first time in the ballot box through their new-found empowerment and self-determination.

Mick has built relationships with businesses that don't just buy from WildHearts but actively champion its cause, unlocking new opportunities that otherwise could have remained hidden from view. Leaders at the American healthcare multinational Johnson & Johnson pushed the WildHearts team to dig deeper into some of the educational challenges faced by girls in rural African contexts. It turns out that in many communities, a third or more of female pupils stay home during their periods because they don't have a way of managing them for class. WildHearts therefore set about working with Johnson & Johnson to access reusable sanitary pads and then it coordinated with its local partners in office-document storage in Africa to piggy-back the routes their vans take, criss-crossing across rural communities every day, to deliver these pads on their rounds, thereby ultimately saving millions of pounds of delivery costs and making otherwise impossible operations widely accessible.

Mick launched WildHearts with an international vision, but he also recognises the need to work at home. In the United Kingdom, other organisations are already specialised in offering inclusive access to finance, and Mick saw no need to replicate their efforts. Mick argues that social exclusion nevertheless remains because it is substantially driven by a 'postcode lottery', which leaves young adults in disadvantaged areas too often without the knowledge, relationships and inspiration they need to break out of endemic cycles of poverty. WildHearts has therefore developed programmes to teach entrepreneur-ship to corporate executives twinned with matching programmes that it makes available for free to school children, often in some of the most under-privileged areas of the coun-try, by using the funding earned from its commercial clients.

WildHearts' corporate training programmes empower professionals to change their perspective of business, create a positive social impact and enjoy a more accomplished career at the same time. The training has reached leaders in businesses from Barclays to Zurich and Nestlé, and in turn this has funded versions of these programmes that have been completed by over 50,000 children in the UK and internationally. The programmes have now been taught in Cambridge and Yale Summer Schools and have won the prestigious Babson prize for entrepreneurship. They have been incorporated into fast-track pathways to apprenticeships and other corporate programmes that have made management opportunities avail-able to young adults, many of whom would otherwise likely have lacked any viable entry into such gainful employment. The training also inspires young people to launch their own ventures that enhance their local communities. As Mick relates, the children 'light up at the prospect of making business mean-ingful' and have pioneered such initiatives as repurposing their school bus during the hours it isn't used to bring senior citizens from surrounding neighbourhoods into school IT facil-ities, where the pupils can teach them computer skills.

Without taking any money from governments or soliciting donations, the drive to upgrade the purpose of enterprise has made it possible for Mick to reimagine entrepreneurial endeavour as a vocation and restore the intrinsic dignity of work. Divergent activities, from supplying uniforms and office furniture to training leaders and providing menstrual products, have all become part of a mission to repurpose resources and re-imagine the role that enterprise can play in people's lives. Mick has not only repurposed his own enterprise activity, but has also inspired executives to think differently about responsible business, empowered children to think differently about their futures and the roles that they can play in their communities, and made it possible for people to harness the power of business to improve their own life chances and those of their peers. As Mick tells me, 'We can imbue any business with meaning. Even a bad day at the office can save lives.'

The opportunity to repurpose isn't limited to governments, charities or even to social enterprises, such as WildHearts, that use their profit to fund social mobility. It holds the key to changing every aspect of everything we do, no matter the sector we operate in or the scale of the enterprise. In fact, as we shall see, it is often in mainstream commercial businesses where the greatest opportunities are overlooked, the greatest vulnerabilities thereby accrue and the most value is therefore left on the table for both the business and its stakeholders. Any business can gain from being genuinely useful to the world it serves; from providing work that is intrinsically rewarding and of societal benefit, or from unlocking forms of economic progress that powerfully engage its stakeholders. And while in Mick's case it clearly helped, there is no requirement to face the bleak conditions of a mountain to find the inspiration!

The Purpose Upgrade

Purpose is the reason why we act in the first place. It defines the outcomes that we seek to achieve. It is not set in stone but can be elevated at any time in response to changing circumstances. When an enterprise lacks purpose, it becomes futile. A Purpose Upgrade is an approach to redirecting, protecting and increasing the value that an enterprise creates through intentional change. It can be applied to repurpose and revitalise individual activities within an enterprise, the enterprise as a whole and, perhaps most importantly though most frequently overlooked, the greater world of activities undertaken outside the enterprise, including by its customers and partners.

A Purpose Upgrade should serve to integrate and align the purpose and actions of an enterprise with the aims and aspirations of its stakeholders. This holds the key to growing our enterprises more effectively by better meeting the needs and priorities of our stakeholders as they arise and for the long term. And it opens the door to unprecedented levels of support from outside the enterprise by harnessing the power of shared ambition.

Purpose focuses our attention, enabling us to make progress. Over time, however, that very focus can work against us, as what was previously a useful lens through which to view our activities turns instead into a dangerous set of blinkers, blinding us to the implications of external change. Too often we fail to recognise the need for a Purpose Upgrade or fail to identify the best way to go about it because we have become trapped by our prior perceptions, assumptions, routines and expectations. This masks the potential for our most extraordinary achievements and holds us back from embracing our greatest future. We can overcome this challenge, however, by discovering how a Purpose Upgrade can be achieved and by putting it into practice as a new capability.

Change your business to save the world

As Mick's example demonstrates, business can provide a powerful means to turn creativity into positive change. Enterprise is born in the recognition of need and the capacity to meet that need. But in recent decades business has too often overlooked true human need. As Professor Tim Jackson, former Chair of the UK's Sustainable Development Commission, put it to me, 'We have fostered a consumerism that engages us in spending money we don't have to create impressions that don't last, on people we don't care about.' Businesses have pursued ever greater specificity within existing industry norms, cancelling out each other's offerings through forms of competition that limit success by burrowing ever more deeply into existing assumptions that too often extract rather than create value. We have food businesses that impoverish the land and cause obesity; financial services that get us hooked on unaffordable credit; pharmaceuticals companies that focus more on yield management than innovation; social media platforms that amplify fake news and abuse; and fossil fuel businesses responsible for the vast majority of the carbon emissions that now place more lives in danger than any other activity in history.

In a 1927 edition of the *Harvard Business Review*, Wall Street Banker Paul M. Mazur argued that businesses needed to move from addressing needs to desires. Ironically, there is now a vast opportunity to step back and prevail by meeting the deeper needs of our customers and other stakeholders. We can succeed not by overlooking the broader context of their lives but rather

14

by embracing it. The need to address the climate emergency to keep our shared home safe. The need to preserve and restore the biodiversity on which our lives depend. The need to overcome poverty and include more people in the benefits of economic change. The need to tackle loneliness, maintain mental health and wellbeing, foster meaningful relationships and negotiate a rapidly changing world in which 'normal' is susceptible to constant reinvention. Each of these needs can be supported at greatest scale and in the most lasting ways through forms of enlightened enterprise.

Living standards have been estimated to have risen over 10,000-fold since the birth of capitalism.[1] While such analysis begs many questions, in whatever way we assess the benefits of modern living, the gains we have made are not guaranteed to further increase or even to last into the future without intentional leadership, and many people in all countries are now experiencing a hardship imposed by inequalities and resource shortages.

While over 700 million people, or 10 per cent of the global population,[2] still live amid conditions of extreme poverty, meaning that they have an income of less than the equivalent of 1.90 dollars per day, the most powerful way to end that poverty is through decent work.[3] The global population is estimated to rise to 9.7 billion by 2050,[4] creating a need for business to foster sustainable agriculture and provide nutritious solutions that can reach us all. Maternal health and the empowerment of women around the world depend on the products and hiring practices of businesses who in turn can benefit from improving the freedom and economic circumstances of half their customer base. Over 2.4 billion people need better access to water, which businesses can address through better stewardship and innovation. Responsible investment can align business priorities with global challenges and over 1,500 investment institutions with approximately sixty-two-trillion-dollar assets under management have already signed up to the UN-backed Principles for Responsible Investment.[5]

If you want to change the world, there may be no greater lever to pull than to find a solution to a problem and to deliver and scale that solution through meaningful enterprise. In so doing you can make life easier, more complete, more worthwhile and perhaps even more magical for the people whom you reach. Rarely if ever has the scale of the opportunity to make a difference been greater.

Change the world to save your business

There is also a powerful argument to suggest that enterprises will better succeed in their own terms by aiming at something bigger than their own benefit. We are most likely to prosper by first creating value for others which in turn leads to our own greater reward. Empirical evidence substantiates the premise.

Alex Edmans has built perhaps the most robust evidence-based business case for purposeful enterprise so far, with a meta-analysis showing that enterprises out-perform their peers by seeking to create a social value of which they retain a portion in profit rather than seeking to maximise profit directly.[6] Purpose can serve to unlock greater agency from all an enterprise's stakeholders, uniting them in a collective pursuit that makes them all better off. 'To reach the land of profit,' Edmans has told me, 'we must follow the road of purpose.' In one study he undertook, businesses that were better to work for delivered stock returns that out-performed their peers by a cumulative 89 per cent to 184 per cent over a twenty-eight-year period.[7] Purposeful businesses unlock superior processes of change and build better partnerships.[8] They can also enjoy better relationships with investors through better engagement and more integrated reporting. *Forbes*'s 'JUST 100' companies, ranked highest in the US on purpose and contribution to society, for example, achieved 56 per cent higher shareholder returns over five years than the hundreds of other businesses ranked below them.[9] This explains why current investment flows are already being directed on a massive scale to more sustainable opportunities with future investment activity forecast to increase this trend at an accelerating rate.[10]

Researchers have identified compelling evidence that customers are considerably more likely to try,[11] stay loyal to,[12] pay more for[13] and advocate for[14] products from purpose-driven companies. This effect is even more pronounced among younger generations. A strong purpose improves strategic clarity by defining a territory for growth;[15] improves corporate reputation by aligning with customer values;[16] and strengthens innovation[17] by fostering greater understanding of need. The stronger relationships with customers that purposeful enterprises build ultimately lead to more valuable brands.[18]

Purposeful enterprises benefit from substantially superior employee engagement, finding it far easier to recruit new talent,[19] reduce turnover[20] and mobilise a greater engagement for any given level of salary.[21]

Purposeful enterprises may also be more likely to find themselves on the right side of changes to legislation, by better factoring in their 'negative externalities', the economic term for the costs of their operations that are (at least temporarily) borne by society rather than the business. It has been estimated that regulation can place as much as 30 per cent of the value of publicly traded corporations at stake.[22]

In a changing world our purpose must be responsive in order

to remain effective. There is no success to be found in answering only yesterday's questions. Repurposing our enterprises and revitalising the activities within them are a necessary source of renewal without which any business is likely doomed to decline and failure.

For all these reasons, purpose must now become the highest priority concern at every level of an organisation. Never have the most important things also been so urgent. Changing our businesses to save the world is entirely compatible with changing the world to save our businesses.

The Purpose Upgrade in the evolution of enterprise adaptation

In environments of accelerating change businesses learned to innovate, first incrementally through minor variations and then discontinuously, often by combining technologies and ideas from different domains to form new and more advanced propositions.

With the development of the internet and associated technologies, enterprises went further, with processes that reconfigured not just *what* we offer but *how* we offer it. The focus shifted from innovation to transformation.

We are now entwined in each other's fates so deeply that we need to go beyond changing *what* we do and *how* we do it to a more fundamental level of adaptation that comes from changing *why* we take action in the first place. The very purpose we serve must become more context-driven, collective and holistic. We no longer simply need to transform our organisations and institutions. Rather, we need to fundamentally repurpose them.

We are living in the wake of a global health and economic crisis that may cast its shadow for years to come. But the risk of further, potentially more virulent pandemics is increasing. Numerous other problems also face us, from the climate emergency to resource depletion, to international conflict, to a cost-of-living crisis and to types of social fragmentation which threaten to disrupt our lives in ways which could in retrospect make the coronavirus look more like a warning of risk ahead than a one-off disruption to be managed before a return to normality. At the same time, we have arguably more reason to be optimistic than at any previous point in history. We have never had greater technology at our disposal nor been connected to as many opportunities to create value and make a difference.

COVID-19 highlighted the interdependence of today's world and the hidden vulnerabilities that this can create. It showed us that emergent reality can impinge on all of us in surprising ways that call every fundamental into question. But it has also provided an opportunity to reconsider how our greatest needs present themselves and what more we can do to address them. One commentator memorably defined the pause in economic activity during the pandemic-induced lockdowns as 'The Great Reflection'.[23] The nature of our recovery will largely be determined by the quality of the ideas to which we now turn.

The ideas that you use to grow your enterprise may often need to become surprisingly normative.[24] They will require you to choose this over that; to value one thing over another; and to take a stand for the types of change you wish to support and create in situations you may never have previously foreseen.

We cannot escape this, because to take action in today's interconnected and interdependent world is to instigate cascading effects that reach out in all directions, like ripples in a pond when you cast a stone into its centre. It is also to be impacted by the ripples of the stones cast by everyone else.

To become aware of these effects; to change them with purpose; and to mobilise new sources of support from differently engaged stakeholders, will be the basis of a reimagined form of success that not only endures but rises higher with every fresh undulation.

The structure of the book

Part commentary, part call to action and part practical guide, *The Purpose Upgrade* is intended to accompany you on the journey to a greater level of success by reimagining the fundamentals of how purpose can be formed and achieved through enterprise.

The book draws on a wide variety of businesses and the experience and insights of prominent leaders and change-makers, as well as inspiring unsung heroes you've probably not come across before. It seeks to overturn much of conventional management thinking, with findings from a broad range of scientific as well as enterprise-related disciplines. Purpose is most fundamentally a capacity of human thought. We'll therefore draw insight from the evolutionary and cognitive sciences on how purpose drives human perception, intentionality, behaviour and fulfilment. We shall also draw on complexity theory and systems thinking in understanding how our actions take place and are best understood within a broader map of emergent living wholeness, and the challenges and opportunities that this presents. Most importantly, *The Purpose Upgrade* is a story that you will complete for yourself. Reflections are therefore included at the end of each chapter to support you in applying the idea to your own enterprise and there is a chapter dedicated to implementing a Purpose Upgrade across your own organisation.

THE ENTERPRISE OF HOPE

Our journey includes the following stops:

Part One: The Need
1. *The Origin of Purpose*
We'll explore how human purpose is formed, what it means to achieve its fulfilment and how it must adapt in a changing environment. Only by understanding what makes human purpose unique and how it can best work for us can we unlock its greatest rewards. We shall discover that this even has significant implications for our future as a species.

2. *In Search of Lost Purpose*
We'll identify how businesses and other institutions fail to maintain an adaptive purpose and the results of this failure for themselves and the people whom they serve. By understanding the causes and consequences of failing to repurpose in a changing world and exploring how existing approaches to purpose fall short, we can learn to take remedial steps sooner and more comprehensively, tackling root causes rather than relying on ineffective fixes or incomplete solutions.

Part Two: The Model
3. *A State of Emergence*
We set the upper limits of our success when we choose which problems to address in the first place. Finding a better problem to solve adds greater value than better solving a previously defined problem. We'll learn how to move beyond existing models of extractive consumerism, escape the limitations of our prior perceptions, and create more value for our stakeholders, opening the door to a world of greater meaning and value creation.

4. *The Garden of Forking Paths*

Solving better problems requires us to lead a more ambitious journey of change outside as well as inside the enterprise. We'll explore how to create more collectively ambitious narratives of shared purpose that align rather than divide our stakeholders and provide pathways for whole ecosystems of actors to win together rather than lose apart.

5. *The Wealth of Change*

We depend on the active participation of our stakeholders to achieve our greatest success. We therefore gain by defining our success in terms of outcomes which engage and fulfil their greatest aspirations as well as our own. This creates new opportunities to foster shared ambition with our most important potential allies and provides us with a vital source of renewal, enabling us to succeed by making an ever-greater difference to people's lives and livelihoods.

Part Three: The Practice

6. *Purpose Rediscovered*

We'll learn from the first-hand experience and challenges of leaders repurposing and revitalising their organisations in very different industries and in radically diverse contexts. A Purpose Upgrade underpins many of the greatest corporate turnarounds in recent history and we'll explore a number of cases in depth through the eyes of those who have led the way.

7. *Your Purpose Upgrade*

A Purpose Upgrade is an always-available event for any organisation of any size in any sector. We'll highlight the practicalities of improving the full scope of activities in which an enterprise engages through a Purpose Upgrade wherever and whenever it is needed, and we'll pull together a comprehensive approach to implementing a Purpose Upgrade in your own enterprise.

Epilogue: The Art of For

A Purpose Upgrade does not just change our business. It can change our lives; and it can change the world we live them in. Never before has the difference this can make been more consequential.

Relation to my previous work

The concept of *The Purpose Upgrade* builds on my previous book, *Collaborative Advantage: How collaboration beats competition as a strategy for success.*[25] In that work I challenged the conventional strategy of creating Competitive Advantage and proposed a radical alternative in the form of Collaborative Advantage to create better outcomes for business, customers and society.

Collaborative Advantage explored how we can grow businesses more effectively by better harnessing value-creating potential across the environment in which we operate, working *with* customers and other stakeholders rather than just *for* customers and *against* our competitors. It examined how we can better tackle societal problems by more strongly harnessing our collective resources and working with the people we are most looking to support as the primary agents of their own change. And it provided methods and techniques to empower leaders to achieve greater success by mobilising stronger support from outside as well as inside the organisation.

In *Collaborative Advantage* I argued that we should not just focus on the change that an organisation delivers, but rather on the greater and more meaningful change that its customers and other stakeholders use its products and services to create in their own lives and work. This lays the foundation for a step change in ambition.

The Purpose Upgrade now seeks to harness that greater ambition by looking more fundamentally at how leaders, their managers and colleagues can best determine what purpose to pursue in the first place and how that purpose can redefine the change that they seek to drive and revitalise the actions that they undertake in so doing.

By putting a living purpose at the heart of our organisation and serving a greater good, we are also in a better place to create Collaborative Advantage to begin with. My recommendation therefore is to read *The Purpose Upgrade* first and then consider reading *Collaborative Advantage* as a sequel. Once we have identified the greater changes we want to create through our businesses, building Collaborative Advantage can help us to further involve our key stakeholders in achieving those changes with us.

Part One

THE NEED

Chapter One

THE ORIGIN OF PURPOSE

Purpose can unlock our greatest capacity for individual and collective adaptation.

It has profound implications for the kind of success that we each pursue, the quality of our lives and the legacy that we leave to future generations.

The pursuit of purpose is a story of people finding better ways of doing things and sharing those improvements with each other through the narratives encoded in their words, represented in their actions and embedded across their cultures.

These narratives create norms and rapidly become hidden in plain sight because we accept them so completely. But over time this normalisation can work against us, like an invisible bind holding us back.

By consciously choosing to diversify the sources and types of information that we pay attention to, however, we can increase our situational intelligence, uncover fresh priorities and achieve more ambitious outcomes, unlocking life-changing sets of new norms in the process.

As far as we know we are the first species with the capacity to shape our own development and even future evolution with intentionality. Solving problems on

purpose that we have created by accident will be critical to our survival and success amid twenty-first-century challenges.

The emergence of humankind

Homo sapiens has emerged from a four-billion-year process of evolution through which biology has struggled to overcome entropy: the force of life against the law of decline.

According to systems theory, emergence occurs when an entity is observed to have properties that its parts do not have on their own, but which arise when the parts interact in a wider whole. No single atom in my body is alive. And yet I live.

Emergence dictates how we make sense of the world. Our visual awareness is drawn towards change, because change has more impact than stasis on our chances of evolutionary success, for example through the arrival of a new food source or of a potentially life-ending threat. We focus so tightly on the part of our visual field that we are actively 'looking at' that we fail to notice that the quality of vision at the periphery is far less high.[1] In fact, if you try the experiment of holding your eyes perfectly still and gazing at a backdrop with zero motion, such as a wall, you will find that eventually your vision starts to black out altogether. The absence of change removes the priority of continuing to process visual data over other uses of your body's energy.

We interpret change and in so doing create a store of historic evidence that shapes the neural networks of our brains and reconfigures them to notice subsequent change that may further be useful to our survival. What we 'see' today becomes an emergent outcome of what we saw yesterday and are therefore expecting. And the memories in which we store our perceptions as well as the minds with which we process them are not located in individual neurons but arise as a result of the interactions between them.

Our sense of self is an emergence. Our bodies are formed of trillions of cells that are in an ongoing state of renewal; our molecules have already been components of countless other organisms, ranging from plants to dinosaurs; and the content of our minds, as well as the shape of our actions, is mostly acquired directly and indirectly from other people.[2] We construct our 'selves' through the repeated interplay between different parts of our physiology and the environment of people and situations with which we engage. The continuity of the 'I' at the basis of our self-identify may be our most intimate form of fiction.[3] We can re-direct ourselves at any moment.

Our relationships are emergent. A group of people is not the addition of discrete separate predictable components but rather something that forms its own reality as the emergent product of the interactions between its members. We behave differently when together than we do when alone due to the meanings that we create, implicitly and explicitly, with and about those around us. These meanings determine how we judge ourselves, the available courses of action that we perceive, how we predict the likely responses of our peers and how we find fulfilment. We cannot understand ourselves without understanding each other. The group dynamic itself drives the processes that form us.[4]

Economies are of course also emphatically emergent. They are the product of value-creating interactions between agents that can only be understood in terms of interdependence: we cannot become a customer without a business to order from. 'Markets' and other concepts in economic thought do not exist *per se*. They are constructs used to simplify the representation of a teeming multitude of individual but connected interactions, all taking place in a broader living human continuum of emergent change.[5]

And, of course, the society in which all this takes place is itself an emergent phenomenon that acquires its own characteristics through interactions among its members which could not occur among isolated individuals. Society changes us just as we change it. When Margaret Thatcher said, 'There is no society. There are just individuals,' she did not have contemporary scientific understanding on her side. The very words we use to think and communicate and the rituals of life we participate in are borrowed from the society we grow up in. It would likely make more sense to ask if there is truly any such thing as the individual, separate from the wider context from which we emerge.

Homo propositus

The capacity not just to participate in change but to reflect on that change and upgrade it with intentionality is understood to be a defining characteristic of our species. Our conceptual thinking enables us to go beyond instinct in the pursuit of greater and more abstract goals. We attribute intentionality to others in a way that animals do not.[6] We transcend literal representation in seeking a reason why things are the way they are[7] and we apply conscious efforts to creating changes that reach beyond our immediate circumstances.* Purpose does

---

* Some scientists argue that our intentions can ultimately be explained by our biology and that our sense of free will is therefore an illusion. While most scientists still reject this claim, I suggest that we would still be best off establishing the rules and norms that we live and work by as if we did have free will, even if this were illusory, in order to maintain a culture that promotes pro-social behaviour and discourages anti-social behaviour. Purpose can become self-fulfilling.

not just determine our fulfilment, but defines and redefines what fulfilment means in the first place. It is by taking aim that we can act and by acting that we can best discover a fresh aim to pursue.

Purposeful activity can keep us fully alive to the rolling present moment, in a state that the psychologist Mihaly Csikszentmihalyi calls 'flow'[8] and which can spontaneously produce unwavering concentration and energy. This depends on our having enough of a challenge to hold our attention but not so much that we become overwhelmed. Purpose may, however, require a commitment that reaches beyond these moments and demands an effort of will over a longer duration. Often our greatest learning comes from coping at least for a temporary period with a degree of overwhelm, during which we find a way to increase our capacity to cope with greater challenge. With the right reason why, we can summon the determination to exercise a discipline that transcends immediate reward and even states of flow for a longer-term goal which gives meaning to the effort that it requires.

The need for purpose is a core foundation of human mental health and wellbeing.[9] We can suffer depression, disengagement and a collapse of self-esteem when we lack a connection to purpose, in a self-reinforcing cycle of decline.[10] On the other hand, a strong sense of purpose is a powerful coping mechanism,[11] simplifying our decisions and making it easier for us to channel our energy and actions towards productive outcomes[12] in self-enhancing cycles of improved cognition, performance, achievement, satisfaction, health, longevity and contribution to the people around us.[13] A sense of purpose is even more important to us than happiness, because while achieving happiness as an outcome is temporary and internal, purpose connects us to the world beyond ourselves and pulls us forwards.

The problem of purpose

I once heard the comedian Henning Wehn tell the marvellous tale of the infant Hans, from his homeland, Germany.[14]

Hans' parents adored him but a concern awakened in them that he didn't seem to be learning to talk as quickly as his peers. They overlooked their disquiet to begin with as Hans seemed happy enough, but as the months and indeed years went by, they became increasingly distressed. They tried talking to him, encouraging him, coaxing him, everything they could think of, but all to no avail.

Finally, one day after his fifth birthday had passed and the couple had all but given up hope, Hans uttered his first words over his dessert: 'This strudel is a bit tepid.'

'Hans!' his parents exclaimed. 'We had no idea you could talk! Why haven't you said anything before?'

To which Hans matter-of-factly replied, 'Up until now, everything has been satisfactory.'

Purpose is awakened by problems to solve. It is an effect as well as a cause. It is something we discover through active engagement with our environment, not something we reveal purely from within. Without problems we'd have no reason to change, to adapt, to take action or even, like Hans, to speak. The very monologue inside our minds could dissolve while we remain in a state of unified and undifferentiated serenity. There would be no need to separate signal from noise.

But we do have problems to face and it is by leaning into the problems that impinge on us that we find our way. The philosopher Karl Popper said that 'All life is problem solving.'[15] If that is the case, the good news is that we are natural born problem-solvers. And we exercise this ability by telling ourselves stories.*

Purpose moves us

The archetypal problem that we have to solve is the question of where to go. The need to move with intention† is likely the driver that caused our brains to evolve in the first place.[16] Brains are biologically expensive to run and throughout nature all creatures that do not need to move with volition lack them entirely. The sea squid provides a fascinating combined approach. It first moves with volition until it finds an environment

---

* If you count all the choices we make, there must be thousands of them every day, from big decisions such as what to put in the next chapter of your book, to tiny micro-choices such as how much Oatly to put in your coffee. But our lives don't grind to a halt with all this story-telling because we solve the vast majority of our problems with two simple heuristics, or micro-stories, which reduce the chances of our actions going very badly and increase the chances of achieving outcomes that are at least satisfactory. These comprise first of all the story of the past: 'What did I do last time?', and secondly the story of perception: 'What do most other people do?' This explains for example why when I speak to audiences about purpose, people arrive and sit each in an individual chair without thinking rather than, for example, arriving and studying the chairs as if for the first time and identifying that lining up a row of several chairs and lying down on them might be more comfortable. The trouble comes when we face new challenges for which no pre-formulated response is an optimal fit. This can be evident to us; or, more dangerously, it may be hidden to us. The latter explains why people tend to under-react to warnings of dangers they have not previously experienced.

† If you ever watch a traditional marionette performance, the moment when you first suspend your disbelief and the puppet suddenly becomes a character rather than just a limp toy is most likely when the puppeteer starts to pull the strings and brings it to life through a simulation of intentional movement, lending his purpose to the puppet as the drama unfolds. Movement is one of the easiest ways for us to recognise a living being. It is fiendishly hard to replicate intentional movement in a robot.

sufficiently conducive to its needs to be able to end its search and remain in its new home for the rest of its life. When it finds this domestic bliss, the sea squid jettisons its brain, now that it has become surplus to requirements, in order to conserve energy. Its chances of survival can at that point be better increased by lowering its nutritional needs than by maintaining now unneeded cognitive processing power. It bets its future on never needing a Purpose Upgrade!

We are of course arguably far less good at navigating geospatially than many other species, such as migratory birds. But human cognition allows us to navigate a more sophisticated journey through life. Our imagination helps us to trace a seemingly infinite variety of pathways from our remembered past, through our experienced present, to our desired future.

Purpose is embodied, embedded, extended and enactive

Movement requires cognition, and cognition is embodied. As cognitive philosopher Shaun Gallagher puts it, thinking is no more just something that takes place in the brain than flight is something that just takes place in the wings of a bird. When we hear the word 'lick', for example, sensorimotor areas associated with the tongue become activated.[17] Our neural response is dependent on the existence of the body.

Experience is therefore also embodied. The expression that to understand someone we must walk a mile in their shoes is telling. Building empathy through a simple walk together, for example, has been shown in neuroscientific research to provide a powerful basis for conflict resolution.[18] This may also explain why no chief executive should ever stray too far from the shop floor and the practical empathic insight that it offers.

Sometimes our bodies may know more than our rational minds can tell us, and purpose is something latently pre-existing for us to tune into. We invest considerable attention on the psychology of work, but the embodied state from which we think and act in the first place may be an even more fundamental determinant of our performance.

Cognition is not just embodied in ourselves but also embedded in and extended across our environment. As Buckminster Fuller said, 'If you want to teach people a new way of thinking, don't bother trying to teach them. Instead, give them a tool, the use of which will lead to new ways of thinking.' Purpose lives in the actions the environment allows us to take. These are known in design terms as 'affordances'[19] and relate deeply to how we interpret the world and the possibilities we can see for purposeful action in the first place.

A dog does not recognise the small rectangular object in our hands as a mobile phone because it has no sense of how it can be used (I often wonder what a dog thinks may be happening when it is taken for a ride in a car). Cognition is therefore also enactive. We bring our understanding of our environment into being through our capacity to take action in it, and we generate meaning through those actions, imagined and undertaken. We form our purpose in the light of the possibilities to create change that we perceive.

Purpose is thereby a cognitive reconciliation of mind, body and environment in which each component is co-determined with the others. The living connection and the dynamic fit between its parts is key to successful human being. We use it to orientate our path towards the optimal 'better' that we can best reach at any given point in time. As our environment changes, so too must the purpose that we pursue.

Purpose is shared

Purpose is not just useful to us individually. Human eyes have evolved with uniquely prominent sclerae – the whites of our eyes – enabling others to see the focus of our attention and thereby better cooperate with us.

And if narrative is the method that we use to solve our problems, the magic of that cooperation really gets going when we increase the complexity of the problems that we can solve by sharing our stories with each other.

This is perhaps the greatest advantage we have as humans. Apes, for example, may also be good psychologists, as one primatologist commented, but they never get the chance to compare notes, so their insights cannot outlive them or multiply. All learning is therefore lost within individual lifetimes, and apes as a species cannot develop in the way that humans have by preserving learning across generations and ultimately sharing it across remote locations.

We form our purpose with and through our peers. Our uniquely complex language enables us ultimately to develop social constructs such as religions, nations and of course our enterprises. These are all things that don't exist in the same way that a material object exists but are conceptual tools that ultimately allow human cooperation to reach all around the world at a scale unprecedented and unrivalled by any other species.[20] They allow us to reframe our understanding of the environments we find ourselves in and enhance our capacity for change by repurposing the materials available to us towards ever-greater ends.

We are the product of storytelling on so many interconnected levels that we are unaware of most of their influence, most of the time. We are the product of our perception, which is far more of a story of interpretation than we are usually aware of; of our memory of prior perceptions that we re-create when we access them from the 'gist' of an imprint in our minds;[21] and of our inner monologue or self-talk, which determines so much of how we act and what we achieve. We are the product of our conversations with others; of the roles we understand ourselves to be playing throughout the day; of the society and communities that we are a part of, the art we may enjoy and the politics we may be exposed to or engage with. It is no coincidence that the verb 'to act' means both to take action and to play a part. The very notion of becoming a 'person' derives etymologically from the Latin 'persona', meaning an actor's mask and taken to represent a character in a drama. It is through purpose that we become who we are, performing ourselves into being through the narratives that it awakens in us. We rehearse our way into success. And while we may lull ourselves into believing that the roles that we play are fixed, in reality we can choose to uplift them at any moment with fresh intentionality. Our purpose can be as malleable as our imagination.

The purpose of purpose

One of the most enduring conceptions of human happiness and wellbeing is the Ancient Greek concept of 'eudaimonia'. Etymologically, eudaimonia came from the word 'eu' for 'good' and 'daimon', 'spirit', but has come to be understood as 'human flourishing'. The concept sat at the heart of longstanding philosophical debates in Athens concerning the capabilities required to live life well, with varying emphases placed by different thinkers on strengths of body, mind and soul and on rewards of pleasure and virtue. In his Nicomachean Ethics, Aristotle argued that eudaimonia is the meaning and the purpose of life, the whole aim and end of human existence.

The concept of human flourishing still shapes our understanding of wellbeing and a life well lived today, infusing it with notions of agency and social significance as well as satisfaction. It has been applied in various ways by psychologists in models of self-development and actualisation[22] and even to measures of the happiness of populations as a whole.[23]

It transcends the notion of immediate contentedness and has more depth and longevity than, say, the rush of joy that your pet dog may display when you give him a treat. Flourishing isn't just about gratification; it fosters resilience, growth and a concern for people beyond friends and family. It has been described as the opposite of living a life that feels hollow or empty. Developmental psychologist Carol Rhyff labels it a state of 'challenged thriving' that makes the most of our human potential and is indicated by feelings of self-acceptance, meaning and purpose, mastery over the problems and opportunities that confront us, positive relations with others, personal growth throughout life, and autonomy and independence.[24]

Eudaimonia appears compatible with a key principle in nature called 'hormesis', the process through which environmental challenges can provoke us to become more resilient. The old adage 'what doesn't kill you makes you stronger' may convey a guiding force of nature. There is generally a favourable biological response to low exposures to toxins and other stressors. This provides the reason why moderately intense exercise is so beneficial to health, breaking down the body's tissues and other structures and in so doing provoking a repair mechanism that makes them stronger than they were before. It is perhaps unsurprising therefore that living a meaningful, challenged and connected life correlates with better health with increased resistance for example to arthritis, diabetes and cardiovascular disease, as well as to enjoying longer and better sleep.[25] *Eudaimonia* connects us to a type of growth that pulls us into being something greater than we otherwise might have remained.

Eudaimonia also connects to the evolutionary basis of our existence in its emphasis on living within an optimal range of human functioning.[26] An exploration of the biological under-pinning to human flourishing must take us to a natural law that pre-dates humankind by nearly 3.8 billion years to the start of the evolutionary process itself and which is responsible for keeping us within that range of conditions conducive to life: the 'homeostatic imperative'.

Neuroscientist Antonio Damasio explains that homeostasis is a far more dynamic process than we typically realise. Homeostasis has often, perhaps unhelpfully, been compared to the functioning of a thermostat that is used to regulate temperature and maintain it within a set range by turning the heating on each time the temperature drops below a certain floor level and then turning it off again when a ceiling temperature is reached. The homeostatic imperative is infinitely more complex, diverse and adaptive than such analogies suggest. It drives a 'backing and forthing' that allows us to improve our conditions by engaging with change. This may be why, as Nassim Nicholas Taleb has observed, we don't enjoy static air-conditioned temperatures as much as we like the contrast of a warm room with an open window allowing in a gentle breeze.[27] Like a boat sailing into the wind, we 'tack' our way into greater wellbeing, adjusting our direction as we go.

Homeostasis regulates the sense and response mechanisms present at every level of our biochemistry, and it is from its processes that feelings and emotions emerge, providing the motivation for our purpose and ultimately giving rise to and reinforcing the stories that we tell ourselves and others to bring about its fulfilment. The homeostatic imperative gives us insight into what humankind may be said to be for and it supplies a powerful biological rationale for the concept of a Purpose Upgrade, in response to changing conditions.

The fulfilment of purpose

Unlike economists, human beings are not designed to measure in a linear way. Our sense of smell, for example, is logarithmic: as the concentration of the source of a smell increases, our perception of it increases at the opposite of an exponential rate. This makes us great at detecting potentially harmful smells at a low level without them overwhelming us as they increase in intensity. Human hearing is another example of non-linearity. Not only is it non-linear but as with other senses and to a spectacular degree we can tune into it and foreground its keenest capacity to filter and detect particular sources, for example when we hear our name mentioned on the other side of a crowded room.

We are optimisers rather than maximisers because our wellbeing depends more on our overall balance than on the prioritisation of individual factors at the expense of the whole-ness. This explains why, for example, that just as you can have too little of a good thing, so too can you have too much of it. Even an apparently unambiguous good such as hydration can be taken too far. Each year a surprising number of people manage to drink enough water after exercise to inadvertently kill themselves. The more common path of over-consumption not of hydration but of calories is of course the key driver of one of the greatest challenges to health of the western world: obesity.

'Good enough' of everything is more key to human wellbeing than ever 'more please' of one thing alone. Such a balancing effect even relates to the pleasure in the form of happiness that we derive from increasing our wealth.[28] Rises in salary drive increases in wellbeing as they lift us out of poverty and into a level of prosperity in which we can take care of most of our practical needs. But the rewards in happiness per unit of wealth decrease rapidly beyond that, and indeed much of the additional happiness we derive from further gains at higher levels of wealth really comes from the status-validating sense that we are doing well relative to others. Studies show that people would prefer a lower salary, for example, if that salary were far greater than the average, in preference over a higher salary but in conditions in which their salary would actually be low relative to other people's. Our happiness is a question of our interactions with others in context. Professor of economics at the University of British Columbia John Helliwell has undertaken research based on the World Values Survey, taking data from around fifty countries to conclude that just going from being friendless to having one friend or family member to confide in had the same effect on life satisfaction as a tripling of income.[29]

Adaptive and maladaptive cycles

The origin of most cognitive bias or 'thinking error' and our common inability to change in the face of new circumstances lies in how we unconsciously perpetuate the stories and behaviours that solved yesterday's problems.

Change gives rise to fresh purpose but over time our conscious intentions gradually become our unconscious assumptions and our intentional actions turn into our unthinking habits. These habits play a vital role in liberating our conscious minds from routine decision-making for higher-order problem-solving. Our assumptions filter out most of the data that we could perceive so that we can concentrate on those of highest value to us. Our habitual self-replicating patterns of behaviour reduce the cognitive load of action by simplifying our path and allowing us to act on auto-pilot, using less energy than is required to solve problems afresh.

In changing circumstances, however, the most valuable sources of information may themselves change and the filtering mechanism of our assumptions can work against us. The blind spots created by our prior understanding can become particularly harmful when the data indicative of our greatest problems appears far away. Perhaps our biggest threat, the climate emergency, has accelerated most quickly in the Antarctic, out of sight and too often out of mind. The greatest inequalities are also typically found between our 'in-groups' and our 'out-groups' rather than within our own 'in-groups' where we are more tangibly aware of them.[30] The relative distance and invisibility of these challenges contribute to our failure to disrupt the cycles of activity that exacerbate them.

We need the capacity to repurpose our cycles of change to prevent them from turning from positive to negative. This explains the value of questions that help us to bring into sight that which was previously hidden from view; it explains why our best ideas may occur to us when we are away from our desks and out of our usual routines; and it likely provides insight into nature's way of re-initiating our thought patterns during the cycle of day and night.[31]

The purpose of disruption

We are often at our most purposeful when something goes unexpectedly wrong, demanding a completely new course of action and serving a previously unidentified goal.

THE ORIGIN OF PURPOSE

I remember the day my father had a stroke when visiting me from Buckinghamshire. The particular concern was not just that he could have a further stroke in the hours that followed but also that as a heart transplant patient, only a specialist hospital could best provide the needed oversight for his recovery and to prevent additional complications arising from the knock-on effects on the health of his heart. The two-hundred-mile-drive to Harefield Hospital was a taut experience of driving quickly but safely, while trying to keep him awake in case falling asleep would lead to him losing consciousness. Of course, I wish there had been no need for the journey and that his visit had been free of incident. But the memory comes back to me because if I ask myself what purposeful activity feels like, then that journey comes to mind. It contained the key components of adaptive change:

1. **A problem**: The difference between getting him to Harefield safely or not could literally have been a case of life or death. This new understanding entirely eclipsed the prior intention of a morning to relax together.
2. **A solution**: There was something I could do to make a difference and bring about the desired end state, in this case driving to the hospital. If I had been in the passenger seat rather than the driving seat, the memory would have stayed with me just as clearly but I'd have been unlikely to associate it so readily with my own feeling of 'purposefulness'.
3. **An intended outcome:** The goal was to access life-preserving treatment at the hospital.

And of course, as is always the case with human purpose, the destination would not turn out to be just the end of one story but also the beginning of the next, in the form of ways to support recovery and recuperation after the hospital care: a fresh opportunity to repurpose. My actions, and even the far greater actions of the medical teams at Harefield themselves, became parts of a bigger picture. The true recovery came from my father's determination to stay alive for his family and the vigilant care of my mother as they adapted their lives to accommodate any necessary change, repurposing in the light of the further unfolding context.

Breaking the rules

A few years later, when an intensive care nurse asked me to turn off life-support for my father after the complications of his medical history finally caught up with him, I knew it was the right thing to do but was not ready to say the words aloud. Instead of following the rules, she used her judgement in context to take the right action, bringing a higher order of purpose and empathy to her response.

When Stanislav Petrov ran a Soviet early warning centre and received a report of five nuclear missiles heading towards the USSR, he trusted his intuition. He ignored the protocol, convincing colleagues that the reports were a false alarm when he did not yet know that to be the case.[32] He repurposed Soviet response from retaliation to the preservation of peace. It is arguable that no single human act has ever had a greater consequence. You and I may be alive today thanks to him. Without his intervention, the world would have suffered a catastrophic nuclear war. Our need for future Stanislavs, however, may well not be exhausted.

In repurposing we come from a deeper place and become capable of reaching a greater goal. It is in these moments that the greatest opportunities become accessible to us. It is work that makes us irreplaceable by machines.

Creating new normalcy

While our shared narratives can become so seemingly 'normal' that we take them for granted, in truth they are more susceptible to change than we are usually aware of.

For example, if we take the context of disasters and emergencies, the very concept of a 'humanitarian crisis' did not exist through most of history. When fires, plagues or internal conflict struck remote parts of the world, it may have been thought of as bad luck or a dreadful fate for those affected, but did not give rise to a sense that we in our part of the world were in any way responsible for intervening to alleviate the suffering. The notion of the humanitarian disaster or emergency is a social imaginary construct which calls on our shared humanity to take action in a way that has ultimately given rise to the architecture of the humanitarian system[33] and a widespread recognition of the value of all human life.

But just as new narratives can be benign in the new purpose and opportunity that they bring with them to begin with, it is also true that they can hold us back over time. Encoded in the notion of a humanitarian crisis, to continue the example, is the idea that the people affected are unable to help themselves. This is of course a misleading simplification. As a result of this bias, humanitarian work can still too often focus on improving material conditions in refugee camps, for example, rather than on the greater goal of restoring the fuller autonomy of the people living in them, or of seeking out and supporting those who choose to flee to other parts of the world and thereby bypass humanitarian systems in the first place. The purpose of directly alleviating suffering with food and shelter can obscure the more fundamental gains that may come from upgrading that purpose to the more effective and far-reaching pursuit of helping people to rebuild their lives, thereby harnessing their own agency, resources and energy to better ends. Even when this insight is clearly understood by practitioners around the world, the nexus of organisational assumptions, obligations, relationships, flows of investment and dependencies that have been built up around prevailing narratives make it fearsomely difficult to escape them without a full Purpose Upgrade. In many instances, even when refugees are able to settle in a new country, their very status as refugees can prevent them from accessing legal employment, curbing their prospects for self-determination and holding back the economies of their new home by depriving them of the contribution they could make.

To give a different example of how prevailing narratives may change, I am more 'flexitarian' than vegetarian, but I can readily see how society could evolve away from meat eating altogether, in response to both concerns for animal welfare and the compelling need to reduce greenhouse gas emissions associated with intense animal farming. And I could imagine that after a few decades of a society-wide meat-free diet, someone caught eating a bacon sandwich might make whatever would be the equivalent of the front pages of a tabloid newspaper in the 'shocking scandal of a scoundrel who twistedly ordered the slaughter of a pig and then ate it!'.

A similar story could be applied to many other things that we may rarely have previously stopped to question. As global sustainability expert Mike Berners-Lee warns me, driving just three miles in a petrol-fuelled car in a congested urban environment, for example, takes away over ten minutes of human life from the people around us through the toxic effect of the particulate matter that it releases. Air pollution caused by driving already leads to five times more deaths per year in the UK than speeding.[34] It is not so hard to imagine a time therefore in which that drive into town might engender a rather heavier societal opprobrium. Indeed, an increasing number of towns and cities are already aiming to be petrol- and diesel-free.

Ian Goldin, former vice-president of the World Bank, further brings to life for me how changeable the stories we live by can be across populations as a whole, drawing on his time working with President Mandela. He points out that no one today would support apartheid in South Africa despite the fact that a majority of white people in South Africa did support it when it was in place. Our consciousness can change and with it so much of our sense of normalcy.

Many of the things that we take for granted in any form of human organisation as 'just the way things are' can be far more contingent than we realise. Because we've become so familiar with the narratives that drive them that we have relegated them to our subconscious, we no longer truly 'see' them and can therefore no longer question them or challenge them. Yet they can have a profound impact on the kinds of opportunity we can or can't identify in the first place. The creation of new narratives can, however, open the door to radical new purpose.

Our narratives not only represent the world but in so doing can change our prior understanding and bring a fresh perspective to light. 'Information' only 'informs' us if it tells us something new. We pay most attention to stories that surprise us because evolution has primed us to value learning and adaptation. The best stories reveal a discrepancy with our prior model of the world and support us in identifying a revised frame of reference that we can use in making sense of that discrepancy and taking action accordingly.*

Propositus populi

The shared purpose that we foster, spread and normalise across society even has implications for our future evolution.

As Dennis Dutton puts it in *The Art Instinct*, the 'Darwinian process of self-domestication introduces a place for consciousness and purpose which is absent in principle from natural selection. To that extent Homo Sapiens is a self-designed species.'[35]

We are the first creatures to become aware of our own evolution and to have the reach and capacity to actively change its course through deliberate action (as well, unfairly, as the capacity to impact to an existential degree on the evolution of so many of our fellow species). Indeed, there is already evidence that human culture has accelerated the adaptation of our genes[36] even before we consider the potential implications of genetic modification, trans-humanism or – likely most importantly of all – creating changes in our environment that increase, or in the case of the climate emergency substantially reduce, its habitability at a global scale.

Past performance is not always an indicator of future success. We have cultivated human purpose to upgrade life in powerful ways that have greatly accelerated in the relatively recent history of the past few hundred years. But we have already

---

* One reason we may 'fast-forward' or 'skip' adverts is that unlike the shows they interrupt, they usually lack the capacity to surprise us and thereby fail to arouse our curiosity. Perhaps if advertisers programmed in the occasional unexpected 'rogue' advert telling us something they wouldn't usually want to share, then their campaigns might capture more of our attention.

made catastrophic mistakes including two world wars. Our distinct capacity for purpose has made us uniquely successful among species. But that capacity could become maladaptive if we do not redirect it to meet the needs of our times.

Prior populations have struggled to repurpose collectively when faced with radical environmental change. As Paul Behrens among others identifies,[37] there are cautionary examples to be found among ancient civilisations that faced radical resource depletion and/or climatic change accompanied by increases in social complexity that made it hard to adjust to a changing environment. The Ancient Sumerians developed both agriculture and irrigation, the success of which enabled their population to grow to a peak of perhaps a million by 2900 BCE. But their irrigation systems lacked proper drainage, which led to an accumulation of salt from evaporated water that rendered their soil infertile. Not wishing to do without the produce of agriculture to which people had become accustomed led to conflict over increasingly scarce yields, ultimately causing a collapse of Sumerian civilisation. A thousand years later the Roman Empire collapsed as its model of slave-labour-dependent inequality became too vast and unwieldy to maintain. The Ancient Mayans did manage to adapt to a number of environmental crises but eventually succumbed to an intense period of deforestation, soil erosion and drought. The Ancient Nazca in Peru met their demise after replacing trees with crops, without realising that trees were necessary to prevent soil erosion, leaving them exposed to floods. And the Greenland Norse met their fate when they were unable to let go of their cattle-based lifestyles and livelihoods as an expansion of ice made them unviable.

We ourselves now face environmental challenges at a global scale as man-made climate change disrupts the conditions necessary for human life to flourish, and as the carrying capacity of the earth is unable to keep pace with the resource demands of its human inhabitants, multiplying threats and increasing the potential drivers of conflict. We also face rising inequalities that threaten our cohesion, technologies that outstrip our capacity for anticipation and control, and exposure to the ever-present threat of sudden changes in financial, economic and social conditions that can reach right around the globe at ever-accelerating speed.

Bringing a Purpose Upgrade to life as we know it may be the most abundant path to ensuring our own wellbeing and to making a contribution that makes our lives significant as well as successful. The only way we can achieve this at scale is through enterprise and organisational life. This is therefore a challenge to the world of business to address our most valuable needs and priorities and to succeed by making a bigger difference.

In the coming chapter we shall explore how organisational purpose can become maladaptive in a changing world, the consequences that this can have, and what is needed to put it right.

We don't have long to tell our story.

For your enterprise

- **What assumptions do we base our actions on? When should we challenge them and how?**
- **What are the cues that we most condition ourselves and the people we serve and work with to notice? Are these the right signals to focus attention on?**
- **What blind spots may we be creating for ourselves and others? How should we overcome them?**

Chapter Two

IN SEARCH OF LOST PURPOSE

The conventional capitalist goal of business, to maximise shareholder value, does little to support leaders in making any of their most important decisions. It tells them nothing about what line of business to enter, what products and services to develop, how to market themselves, or how to navigate a changing operating environment.

Environmental and social governance (ESG) frameworks, corporate social responsibility (CSR) strategies, brand purpose models and alternative forms of enterprise structure fall short of giving leaders a toolkit for addressing their primary challenges in redirecting their core operations.

Businesses' own mission statements and approaches to purpose and planning can also be made insufficient, irrelevant or even actively counter-productive by changing circumstances and the emergence of unforeseen needs and opportunities.

Situational change also puts immense pressure on conventional approaches to governmenmental, democratic and political purpose. At the macro-economic scale, pursuing economic growth, without regard for the nature, purpose and quality of that growth, for how its benefits are spread, or for the wider impacts that it creates, is becoming more obviously hollow as well as, in many economies, simply harder to achieve. And many of today's problems do not fall easily across pre-existing party-political divides.

Civil-society organisations are often the most focused of all on the vulnerabilities that change can bring. But due to limited resources their business models can break at the very moment when their services are most needed, forcing them to seek new forms of collaboration, partnership and engagement to achieve their goals through forms of shared purpose that reach beyond the voluntary sector and involve business and government alongside them.

Individuals too find that the success of their work and ability to achieve a life situation that meets their aspirations increasingly depends on their capacity to repurpose their aptitudes and skills in completely new ways, which can also be empowered by the actions of business and government.

Achieving a Purpose Upgrade may now, therefore, be the most important capability to develop in organisational life, as it is for human life as a whole as we recover from the pandemic and prepare for the challenges ahead.

Capitalism

Fifty-six per cent of people across the major western markets now believe that capitalism does more harm than good.[1] Our current form of economic activity is driving the climate emergency, a reduction in biodiversity and the depletion of environmental resources, as well as increasing significant inequalities, some of which have now reached obviously unjustifiable extremes.

We face what the UN's Secretary General described ahead of COP26 as a 'code red' climate emergency[2] with businesses contributing the overwhelming majority of greenhouse gas emissions. Biologists now believe we are entering the first 'mass extinction event' since the loss of the dinosaurs.[3] And Oxfam found before the pandemic that the world's twenty-six richest people now have more wealth than the bottom half of the population of the world altogether.[4] That figure has since dropped to the world's twenty richest people as the impact of the pandemic has further exacerbated divides.[5] As Ian Goldin has told me, for example, while 1.6 billion people suffered losses to their livelihoods during the pandemic and 400 million people lost their jobs entirely, if Jeff Bezos gave every single Amazon employee a $105,000 bonus, he would still be wealthier now than he was when COVID-19 first struck, after lockdowns increased the online retailer's revenues by $10,000 per second.

Speaking in the House of Commons on 11 November 1947, Winston Churchill coined the phrase, 'Democracy is the worst form of government except for all those other forms that have been tried.' While it could be tempting to make a similar claim about capitalism as a form of economic organisation, we have collectively used the capitalist model to improve human experience on earth beyond recognition. Contrary to any romanticism of bygone idylls, it could be argued that we have achieved more to alleviate suffering and advance human development in the past 300 years than in the prior 200,000 years of our existence. As Steven Pinker maintains,[6] and whatever the newspaper headlines may be, it is almost certainly better to be alive today, on average and for most people, than at any previous time in history. Capitalism is the predominant economic system through which this value has been created. Were it even possible, to bring capitalism to an end would be to turn our back on one of the greatest boons that we have ever created. But capitalism as currently practised is in great need of a Purpose Upgrade.

While the control of trade by private owners for profit has been a tremendous engine of liberty and inventiveness, the catch is that there is no guiding intelligence within this purpose to take into account the broader context in which it operates unless we provide it: perhaps, from this perspective, it is as much 'Daft Kapital' as 'Das Kapital'.

There is also an intrinsic bias in the notion of capitalism to orientate economic activity to favour the intentions of one category of people: those with capital to invest. It is perhaps unsurprising therefore that capitalist systems, left unchecked, tend to increase inequalities over time as ownership of capital creates opportunities for further increasing that capital, creating exponential differences in wealth.[7]

Ultimately, capitalism becomes self-defeating, even in its own terms if those inequalities come eventually to threaten the goodwill on which its freedoms depend, or if the pursuit of profit destroys broader value, including nature's own systems, which provide essential services for humankind to flourish in the first place.

Capitalism doesn't really discover and fulfil human need *per se*. Rather it is an ingenious mechanism to find out what people are willing and able to pay for. While this is extremely useful, it can thereby overlook many of our most fundamental drivers of wellbeing. The old adage that the best things in life are free is a partial truth. The best things in life may be free at the point of enjoying them, but we do have to pay for them through the choices that we make, in our lives, across our communities and through our institutions. If our social fabric becomes torn, capitalist endeavour may be held back or even become impossible. We need a healthy capitalism in a healthy society on a healthy planet.

Capitalism as currently practised is therefore a partial vehicle for solving our problems. Where it too often falls short is in a lack of purpose able to take full account of the situation in which it operates, and it thereby fails to involve and engage the fullest possible support and cooperation.

Shareholder Value Maximisation

A lack of situational intelligence is manifest in the most famous application of capitalist theory to the purpose of the corporation, known as the 'Friedman Doctrine' or 'Shareholder Value Maximisation' (SVM) after the economist Milton Friedman.

In an essay for the *New York Times* in 1970, Friedman argued that 'there is one and only one social responsibility of business – to use its resources and engage in activities designed to increase its profits'.

The proposition has become pervasive in the financial community and much of the business world[8] and in 2016 the *Economist* magazine still described it as 'the biggest idea in business'.

When the accumulation of financial gain becomes a decontextualised aim in its own right, however, rather than a means to a greater goal that takes account of the situations in which we find ourselves, organisations can become inward-looking and overly self-oriented. And unlike humans who will eventually stop eating when they are full, unrestricted capitalism will continue to consume our resources with no end to its appetite.

It is perhaps no surprise that a goal that enshrines the primacy of self-interest in the very statutes of business should eventually lead to collapses in trust from the public, low levels of employee engagement[9] and high levels of negative externality on a global scale. This is a problem for business as much as for society. For example, disengaged employees cost US businesses alone between $400 and $500 billion dollars per year.[10] The phenomenon is reflected in the notion of 'bullshit jobs', a label used by the late anthropologist David Graeber to refer to jobs where the very person doing the job believes it to serve no purpose.[11]

In reducing the purpose of a firm to such a constricted view of its value, Shareholder Value Maximisation overlooks the very basis on which a firm can be legitimately supported by the society that it depends upon: namely that its operations make a greater contribution to humankind than they cost it.

The pervasiveness of the concept of Shareholder Value Maximisation and its consequences should not be underestimated. Powerful ratchet effects reinforce it formally and informally, through everything from company law, to accounting, investor reporting, management practice and employee behaviour. It infiltrates our core assumptions to the point where we lose sight of it just as its effects on our perceptions and actions become greatest. It too often lies in the background, taken for granted, as a powerful unnoticed lens through which we see and understand the organisational life of our businesses, bringing into view one set of possibilities and, just as dangerously, preventing others from coming into view at all.

Unsurprisingly, the doctrine has been criticised by left-wing commentators for impoverishing most citizens at the expense of a corporate elite,[12] and encouraging short-term activities such as buying back stock rather than re-investing profits in a business' future.[13] Perhaps more intriguingly, the idea has also been prominently criticised by many of capitalism's own greatest defenders.

The call for new purpose

As chairman of the largest investment firm in the world, BlackRock, Larry Fink's vision has to extend not just to individual businesses but rather to the value of entire sectors in which he spreads the firm's investments. We can detect enlightened self-interest therefore in his series of open letters to CEOs in which each year he appears to dial up the pressure to move beyond the narrow scope of Shareholder Value Maximisation in the name of longer-term prosperity, integrating a broader range of priorities.

His 2018 letter to CEOs was entitled 'A Sense of Purpose' and in it he argued that 'society is demanding that companies [. . .] serve a social purpose' and that to prosper over the longer term every business must show how it makes a positive contribution, meeting the needs not just of investors, but of customers, employees and communities. In 2019 his letter was entitled 'Profit and Purpose' and he further developed the theme, arguing that 'purpose is not the sole pursuit of profits but the animating force for achieving them [. . .] Purpose guides culture, provides a framework for consistent decision-making, and ultimately, helps sustain long-term financial returns for the shareholders of your company.' And as he reiterated in his letter the following year, 'a company cannot achieve long-term profits without embracing purpose and considering the needs of a broad range of stakeholders'.[14] In 2021, in the midst of the pandemic, Larry pointed out that the re-allocation of capital towards sustainable enterprise had accelerated rather than declined and called on all businesses to disclose plans for their transition to a net zero economy as well as calling for new levels of partnership between government and the private sector with new roles to play for each in effectively repurposing the entire economy. And in 2022, he reiterated that 'In today's interconnected world, a company must create value for and be valued by its full range of stakeholders in order to deliver long-term value for its shareholders.'

It would seem that CEOs have been taking note during the period in which Larry has written these letters. On 10 August 2019, the Business Roundtable issued a new 'Statement on the Purpose of the Corporation', signed by 181 CEOs, including Jamie Dimon of J.P. Morgan Chase (and Chairman of the Business Roundtable), Tim Cook of Apple and Alex Gorsky of Johnson & Johnson, who commented that the statement 'affirms the essential role corporations can play in improving our society'.[15]

The statement publicly commits its signatories, albeit without a mechanism for accountability or clear process for driving change, not only to generating long-term value for shareholders but also to delivering value to customers, investing in employees, dealing fairly and ethically with suppliers and supporting the communities in which they work. It concludes with the observation that 'Each of our stakeholders is essential. We commit to deliver value to all of them, for the future success of our companies, our communities and our country.' Whether we choose to take these claims as sincere or otherwise, their existence demonstrates that these powerful leaders recognise the dependency of their success on the goodwill and participation of all their stakeholders.

Despite such prominent critics, the Friedman Doctrine has hardly become a straw man argument. Indeed, a leader in the *Economist* magazine commenting on the Business Roundtable's

Statement criticised the initiative, describing it as a 'threat to long-term prosperity'.[16] One of the most prominent foundations on which the editorial bases its objections is the notion that 'collective capitalism leans away from change'. The irony of this conclusion comes from the fact that it is change that must give rise to new purpose in the first place. Choosing a purpose without regard to the context in which it is chosen may be compared to choosing a move in a game of chess without knowing where your pieces stand.

The Friedman Doctrine itself was a response to the changing context of its day, in which market liberalisation was leading to a growing number of multi-national and global businesses. The primacy of Shareholder Value and the goal of SVM took hold as businesses scaled and owners became separated from their day-to-day running. Such separation created the so-called 'agency problem', bringing a need for new mechanisms of control to ensure businesses were run consistently with owners' expectations and to ensure an alignment between executives' activity and shareholders' priorities.

The new Statement of the Business Roundtable was in its turn a response to a further changing landscape of accelerating social and environmental problems and also likely a tactical response to assuage potential rising challenges to big business from the Democratic Party. The *Economist* editorial itself concedes that 'workers' share of the value firms create has fallen', 'consumers often get a lousy deal' and 'social mobility has sunk'. As today's world becomes ever more interconnected and interdependent, it becomes increasingly counterproductive to formally isolate and prioritise the interests of one group against the interests of the others on which it depends.

Shareholder Value Maximisation imposes a linear financial logic in which more is always better, and each unit of more adds the same degree of better. And it removes the context of our transactions: the very thing that gives them meaning in the first place. As we have seen, people, on the other hand, like nature of which they are a part, are context-driven and optimisers rather than maximisers. You have almost certainly never met an individual who could live their own life taking every decision on the unique basis of maximising their wealth without regard for the broader consequences of doing so. Such a policy would not even be good for the individual's own self-interest. It would alienate everyone who could help them to succeed and enjoy life. This applies to businesses as well. Too tight a focus on only undertaking activities that we know in advance to be profitable eliminates the far greater range of activities that we can undertake to be useful to our stakeholders and through which we may uncover opportunities for profit as a consequence. Empathy can become a valuable tool for value creation.

As I argue throughout this book, where change leads to the innovation of what we offer and deeper change drives the transformation of how we offer it, the deepest changes require us to adapt at the level of purpose. Capitalism can only work when enough people are willing to buy into its rules and to the degree that they commit their talent, efforts and resources to doing so. Faced with immense challenges, it is now time to raise our game and to find the right alternatives to the forms of capitalism that have been practised up till now.

Individual businesses

Shareholder Value Maximisation is a problematic goal for the leaders of individual businesses. While maximising shareholder value may appear to be of benefit to investors, in separating objective from context it provides no specific purpose to the particular businesses they invest in and certainly not one capable of helping its leaders to drive particular processes of value creation. Trying to maximise value is like trying to maximise success in some abstract and generic way without any consideration of what field you want to succeed in.

Business leaders try to navigate this problem by formulating mission statements that codify the purpose of a business in its own terms within an industry or set of industries. But if these mission statements are subordinate to a greater goal of shareholder value maximisation, they are not the true drivers of the overall change that the business creates and can frequently be met with scepticism. And even when a worthwhile mission is identified, it may need to be upgraded in the face of important change, lest it come to hold a business back from making a valuable new contribution to its stakeholders.

A company may need to change direction because demand for a business proposition falls away. It is quite difficult to pursue any kind of sustainable purpose in the lamplighting, videocassette recorder repairing, leech collecting or (sadly for the early risers) the knocking up trade.*

It may need to repurpose because the use of its products is found to be harmful. When Edward Bernays coined psychoanalyst A.A. Brill's phrase 'Torches of freedom' in 1929 to

---

* 'Knocker uppers' earned a living by tapping on workers' windows to wake them during the industrial era before workers had alarm clocks. One challenge of knocking up was the risk of banging loudly enough on a paying customer's window to wake not only them but also their freeloading neighbours. The knocker uppers eventually settled on the use of long thin sticks, with which they were able to knock loudly enough to wake the intended beneficiary but quietly enough to avoid waking anyone else. Apparently the trade persisted in some areas until the 1970s.

describe cigarettes in a campaign to encourage women to smoke in public despite the social taboo restricting the practice to men, the advertising genius may have been proud of his work, riding an early wave of feminism in the United States and promoting cigarettes as symbols of emancipation and freedom. Hindsight, however, casts a rather different light on the value he was really bringing to women.[17]

An enterprise may need to take a more comprehensive approach to purpose as it scales. The biggest businesses in the world have annual revenues greater than all but the very largest economies. At the time of writing, Walmart has a greater income than Spain; Royal Dutch Shell has a greater income than Sweden; and Apple earns more money than Belgium (though its chips are far less tasty). With this scale comes power, influence and a concomitant expectation from the public of increased responsibility.

An enterprise may also need to redefine its purpose to address new opportunities available to it, whether through a merger or acquisition, an addition to the business portfolio, significant new client relationships or the identification of opportunities for innovation that lie outside the existing mission of the business. The leaders of the Dunhill menswear brand may have reason to sleep easier at night for extending Alfred Dunhill's legacy into fashion than the executives at the Dunhill cigarette brand of British American Tobacco.

Ironically, Milton Friedman himself made the observation that 'Only a crisis – actual or perceived – produces real change. When that crisis occurs, the actions that are taken depend on the ideas that are lying around.' Now is the time to upgrade the ideas we live and work by to fit our new realities and to recognise the hidden needs unaddressed by business today in the more significant problems emerging across society. It has become commonplace to cite the lack of trust in capitalism among our younger generations, but, far more significantly, young people are voicing understandably distressing concerns not just about business but for society as a whole. A recent study by the University of Bath polling 10,000 participants across ten countries found that 56 per cent of young adults believe humanity is doomed, the same percentage of all adults whom we saw earlier believe business does more harm than good.[18] We have a lot to turn around.

Existing alternatives

A number of approaches have emerged to restore a more comprehensive approach to purpose and replace Shareholder Value Maximisation. But none so far appears to provide a complete basis for the pursuit of purpose in rapidly and profoundly changing times.

Corporate social responsibility (CSR) efforts may be sincere and useful. Yet their very nature is to be a side-show to the main spectacle of the business. They are rarely accountable for driving the revenue or financial sustainability of an enterprise. They seldom lead to a fundamental redirection of the processes and outputs of value creation or re-align the core business with its operating environment. And they therefore usually fail to lead to breakthroughs for a business's customers or change the model on which the business is based. Too often they are limited to acts of ethical appeasement, taking the heat out of an unsustainable practice here or deflecting attention from the more exploitative dimensions of an enterprise and its supply chains there. They can be criticised for trying to merely compensate for wrongdoing or inattention to broader impacts of the central business activity through ostensible good works elsewhere. Shouldn't social responsibility be baked into a business's core operations rather than tacked on as an extra? And is 'responsibility' the height of our ethical aspirations in the first place, let alone of our core ambitions for value creation?

Environmental and social governance (ESG) investing has risen up the agenda with increases in sustainable finance expected to drive adaptation to climate-compatible forms of economic development. But once again, the concept of ESG can tend to make us think in terms of trade-offs. Rather than providing an empowering purpose that focuses leaders on creating true value, they may simply provide a curb on excess or a tool for avoiding particular impacts such as CO_2 emissions. ESG principles also have little to say about the core nature of a business. This means that anomalies can occur when a business whose operations are counter to the interests of the environment and society can paradoxically appear to achieve a high ESG rating. A study of FTSE 100 companies by Refinitiv Data in 2021, for example, put British American Tobacco in third place overall.[19] Just because a business can be sustained does not mean that it is solving useful problems. Executives find little in ESG measures to actually help them make their core business a success in terms of how they define and create value. There will always be a limit on the change we can create unless we engage fundamentally with the reason why we are creating change in the first place.

Stakeholder capitalism has emerged as a more integrative concept and speaks to the goals adumbrated by The Business Roundtable and expressed in Larry Fink's open letters. Stakeholder capitalism seeks to create benefits for all the stakeholders of a business and widens the lens on value creation which can lead to improved outcomes for a broader range of groups. A key challenge for stakeholder capitalism, however, is that it may also too often be viewed as a means to balance the potentially conflicting interests and priorities of different stakeholder groups rather than to unlock a new generative purpose for the enterprise. On its own, an awareness of stakeholder needs and potential impacts is not enough to repurpose an organisation. In practice, existing approaches to stakeholder capitalism can therefore tend to reinforce incumbent approaches to business purpose, with an additional mitigation of harmful wider social impacts and enhancement of wider positive social impacts. It may be like trying to spend less time in the office and more time with family: the balancing effect may be important but still does not on its own change the core nature of what you do at work and whether fundamentally it is contributing to lives well lived. The greatest gains from stakeholder capitalism can only be achieved through generative purpose that increases the value that can be created by uniting stakeholders in a better shared endeavour to begin with, growing the total value created as well as dividing it more fairly.

Brand purpose has become a focus for marketing professionals who seek to imbue their brands with meaning that sets them apart. Brand purpose may be focused on questions of customer experience or may include broader ethical dimensions such as brand advocacy on social issues. Because brands represent the facet of business value most exposed to the outside world, they are often also at the leading edge of business response to change. The catch, however, is that brand purpose alone does not always set the agenda for the total change that an organisation brings about, and when there is an apparent misalignment between the two, trust is lost and value destroyed. What credibility does a brand have to campaign on social or environmental issues, for example, if the business behind it is doing everything it can to sell products that deplete our natural resources or to avoid paying taxes that would contribute to resolving the problems that it is campaigning on in the first place? When a business communicates a new purpose through its brands, but this purpose does not drive a change in the problems the business solves, the role it plays in its stakeholders' lives or the outcomes that it ultimately achieves, it is susceptible to the charge of 'purpose-washing': simply pretending to be better than it is.

Social enterprise and **other alternative organisational forms** address the core structure and accountability of business but are often limited to particular types of purpose. They do not necessarily offer universal models that can be applied by all, though arguably all businesses can learn from them. After all, it would be difficult to trust in a future of 'antisocial enterprise'.

The B Corp movement, for example, offers a certification process that businesses can adopt to achieve third-party verification of high standards of social and environmental performance, public transparency and a legal accountability to balance profit and purpose. Cooperatives are also a form of enterprise that share ownership across their members, whether they are a consumer cooperative or a producer cooperative. More than one in ten people on planet earth are members of a cooperative[20] and the cooperative movement has achieved many ethical and economic successes, often providing unusually stable employment and fairer conditions. But once again, while being a certified B Corp, another form of social enterprise or a cooperative plays an important part in rooting purpose in high ethical standards or shared ownership, the adoption of these legal structures does not in itself guarantee that an enterprise is pursuing an optimal purpose through its core value creation processes. A business may even end up achieving less by diluting its capabilities in pursuit of too broad a range of measures in following generic approaches to ethical performance rather than on concentrating on the issues where it can make the biggest difference through its own particular capabilities.[21]

The ostrich approach to leadership, or 'business as usual' is, paradoxically, likely to be both the most universally derided and yet most widely practised approach. A widespread cognitive failing in organisational life has been dubbed 'plan continuation bias':[22] a tendency to continue with a course of action that is no longer viable or optimal as we attempt to fulfil our prior expectations and those of the people around us. Perhaps the greatest lack of change comes from the cumulative effects of self-reinforcing feedback loops that keep us locked in maladaptive responses, including everything from the power of individual habit to peer influence, culture, professional norms and even regulatory frameworks. Whatever the cause of the approach, 'business as usual' will not address the global challenges to which we are all exposed and will benefit no one in the long run. And that long run seems to catch up with us more quickly each year that passes.

Giving up and starting again may be seen as an attractive option to the more revolutionary-minded. But however strong our appetite for change, our lives are usually too dependent on the capabilities already in existence to step outside the system completely and simply begin afresh.

As Ian Goldin puts it to me, 'Without a short term there is no long term.' Individual businesses must make transitions to new purpose that enable them to maintain existing employment where possible (or support colleagues in transitioning to new roles), and harness the capabilities that they already possess as well as investing in new opportunities.

Similarly, at the macro scale, utopian visions quickly become irrelevant to most people's lives or, worse, turn to cruel realities when there is a disconnect between the vision and a workable pathway to collective success.

We therefore need to make greater use of our existing productive capacity and open the door to more comprehensive, viable transitions to greater purpose. This means repurposing our existing capabilities rather than assuming that they must be abandoned altogether.

We have become familiar with repurposing on a temporary and limited basis as companies such as LVMH repurposed their factories to produce hand sanitiser and car manufacturers repurposed assembly lines to manufacture ventilators during the COVID-19 pandemic. And during the invasion of Ukraine we saw businesses re-direct their activities altogether to provide an immediate response, ranging from sheltering people fleeing the conflict to distributing provisions and even military equipment. But while repurposing a whole business at a potentially global scale and for a lasting future is a challenge, there are already enterprises that can demonstrate its revolutionary potential — as we shall discover.

The road to purposeful enterprise

Initiatives are now emerging to support the development of purposeful enterprises. These include The Purposeful Company in the UK, which seeks to use evidence to influence policies that support long-term value; the British Academy, which identifies priorities for research and public engagement with purpose, promoting changes in legal definitions of corporate purpose as well as influencing regulation, investment, governance, finance and performance measurement; and the Coalition for Inclusive Capitalism in the US which highlights investor and reporting practices that support purpose and identifies principles for creating more opportunities for workers, expanding the workforce and enabling fair gain-sharing. The United Nations has also sought to empower businesses around the world to integrate their Sustainable Development Goals into enterprise purpose by enabling businesses to align their purpose with specific global priorities of relevance to their activities among the 17 goals and 169 targets intended to address poverty, hunger, health, education, gender equality, water and sanitation, clean energy, work and economic growth, innovation and infrastructure, reduced inequality, sustainable cities and communities, responsible consumption and production, climate action, life on land and underwater, and peace and justice needs of the world. These initiatives provide important guidance and contribute to a more enabling environment, but they also raise many questions. Leaders and their colleagues will have to determine how they can they make the shift to purposeful enterprise in their own context and as the basis for ensuring the excellence of their own operations as well as maintaining a dynamic fit over time between their purpose and an ever-changing world.

Government

The need to repurpose is not limited to private sector enterprise. Just as our assumption that the role of business is to increase wealth for its owners, overlooking the contribution it must make to other stakeholders and paradoxically succeeding less even in its own terms as a result, we also tend to assume misleadingly reductive roles for government to play. As the economist Mariana Mazzucato argues persistently and compellingly,[23] when we see the economic role of government as merely to correct market failures and enable other sectors to create value, we unwittingly hide many of the greatest contributions government can make in a blind spot created by these assumptions. This can lead to a cumulative impoverishment in the competence and capabilities to be found within government, unnecessarily limiting the contribution that it can make to the public good. Government does not have to restrict itself to passing laws and imposing taxes to achieve its aims but it can play a role in innovation and in engaging society in voluntary change.

Furthermore, through their responsibility to provide services that reach right across society to the most vulnerable, governments are perhaps more exposed to many types of change than business, which can leave their initiatives misaligned with real needs. And perhaps precisely because much of their activity is not included in predominant measures of a nation's wealth, we often do not perceive the full role they already play in value creation or appreciate the full purpose that they can serve. The net contribution to the economy when integrating all impacts can be greater for many public sector activities than it is for many businesses. Failing to understand this can limit investment and restrict our vision of what is possible.

To match the scale of today's problems we should seek to better integrate the public sector with the change-creating potential of business and the participation of citizens in collective action with shared purpose that reaches and involves us all. We need our states to become more entrepreneurial just as we need businesses to become more responsible and inclusive. The mathematics of cooperation are not additive but multiplicative. Widening the lens on the benefits we seek to create opens the door primarily not to a redistribution of benefits but to the creation of greater overall prosperity. This may often require new relationships and the creation of new forms of commitment and trust.

Democracy and political parties

The need to repurpose is fundamental to democracy. The US Constitution is cherished as a democratic milestone and the foundation of the Free World, yet it allowed slavery and refused the franchise to women, both of which would be unconscionable today.*

Democracy faces increasingly complex challenges. The power of the individual state is diminishing relative to the global economy. The very spread of the COVID-19 virus and its variants around the globe is but one revelation that the national boundaries of democracy are porous.

A dislocation in the face of such deep change has arguably led to a loss of clear purpose among political parties in many parts of the world. Today's political parties were often forged in yesterday's battles. The left–right divide, like capitalism and the Friedman Doctrine, shares the limitation of representing individual factions rather than society as a whole. In the United Kingdom, for example, the Labour Party was founded to get a better deal for working-class people, and much of its funding comes from Trades Unions whose members are one part of

---

* Though tragically, while slavery has been abolished as a legal trade, it continues illegally at a greater scale than at any previous point in history. It is estimated by Anti-Slavery International and others that over forty million people now live in conditions of modern-day slavery. Conditions of crisis and emergency further exacerbate the problem by creating more opportunities for exploitation.

that group.[24] The Conservative and Unionist Party is often considered to represent wealth owners. Owning your own house has long been considered a reliable indicator of a likelihood to vote Tory. Even in the 2019 General Election, in which many people voted Conservative in traditional Labour seats, including in the so-called northern 'Red Wall', the Tories benefited from the votes of elderly owner-occupiers and other home owners. Of the 365 seats won by the Conservatives, 315 had home ownership levels above the national average of 64 per cent, compared with just 53 of the 202 won by Labour, while only three Conservative-electing constituencies had a home ownership rate of less than 50 per cent. And in the May 2022 local elections, Michael Gove told the *Sunday Telegraph* that the subsequent Conservative losses could be linked to falling levels of home ownership in London.[25] The party also draws much of its funding from the contributions of individual high-net-worth backers. At the time of writing, 25 per cent of Tory Party individual donations come from just ten people.[26]

But today's challenges do not fall easily across such party-political and factional divides. In the United Kingdom, Brexit brought the Houses of Parliament to gridlock because parties could not easily align around clear positions. Drawing a clear distinction between government policy and opposition alternatives was also difficult during much of the pandemic.

If we look at the key challenges of the years ahead, such as regulating advances in technology; fostering climate-compatible development; organising for an ageing population; and weathering the storms of changing patterns of international conflict and cooperation, we find that they are cross-cutting issues that do not plot themselves along the current political spectrum and to which today's leaders and processes may often seem under-equipped. Nor indeed can they realistically be solved by prioritising the needs of only certain groups within societies. They are 'everything problems' that require 'everyone solutions'. Political parties will need to find new purpose and will need to do so in the face of rapidly changing and ever more surprising environments. When Boris Johnson became Prime Minister of the United Kingdom, his purpose was to 'get Brexit done'; within weeks, his purpose was to stay alive while in intensive care and to get the nation through the pandemic that put him there and the economic hardship that it would cause.

Politicians cannot assume sole (or even primary) agency for solving any of these problems. The response to COVID-19 required us all to play our parts with vigilance and our recovery from the pandemic as well as our resilience to future shocks can only come from empowering us all to be important change-makers and value-creators. It is only through consensual collective action that we can gain purchase on our biggest challenges.

Civil society

Voluntary activities depend for their very existence on aligning their stakeholders around a common idea for positive change. Without that alignment they cannot function or sustain themselves. Purpose is the currency of the change they bring about in the world.

The voluntary sector is arguably the sector most exposed to a changing world. The human, social and environmental problems civil society organisations address frequently represent the most acute end of emerging problems, from floods to knife crime, or from homelessness to infectious disease.

In many regards the voluntary sector may therefore also be the most exposed to the need to repurpose, addressing as it

73

does the sharpest-edged consequences of social and environmental problems on the front line of where they are most felt among society's most vulnerable groups. Civil society is there to hold us together and to bridge the gaps that may be left by government and business.

More extremely than government, voluntary sector organisations are exposed to the challenge of being dwarfed by the scale of the challenges they exist to address. This means they typically have to work with and through other actors to achieve their goals, defining and redefining their own roles in the process. They choose between direct action to alleviate a problem, advocacy and campaigns to pressure sources of power to effect greater change, or empowering people affected by a problem to better help themselves. By necessity, many non-profits are therefore ahead of their private-sector colleagues in thinking through the challenges, opportunities and nature of forging coalitions of shared interest.

It is unsurprising, therefore, that when voluntary organisations work on their strategy reviews for a new planning horizon, the focus almost always begins with a deep reflection on purpose within the organisation as well as across their stakeholders as the basis for any new direction or strategic pivot. These conversations are not without their tensions. Larger charities have built business models that depend on the nature of the solutions they offer. Identifying more effective pathways to success through greater collaboration often also means identifying a new basis for the sustainability of these operations. New approaches may cannibalise the old. The questions this raises rarely seem easy to answer and often require great courage. But a capacity to repurpose and to support others in repurposing is essential in ensuring that these organisations avoid decline and more importantly make the greatest contribution that they can to enabling the change they seek.

Individuals

The challenge of purpose-led adaptation is not limited to organisations but clearly faces us all. In recent years, with COVID-19 and other crises, we have begun to experience threats to human agency that can feel like an attack on the very status of a human being in the modern world.

The Marmot Review[27] in the UK revealed that the life expectancy of British citizens was already threatened by an austerity that is now exacerbated by a cost-of-living crisis; the so-called Barnet graph of doom[28] indicates that with changing demographics the United Kingdom is heading towards a time when the cost of social care alone will exceed the total budgets of local authorities for all services combined; economists such as Daniel Ritter suggest that globally we have already passed 'peak human wellbeing';[29] and commentators such as Paul Mason describe the 'collapse of the neo-liberal self',[30] as the stories we have told ourselves about how to get on in the world are no longer working, leaving us in a 'scriptless' state in which we don't have a workable concept in our minds that we can use to climb out of our problems.

As we look to the future, the question of whether our work will be supported or undermined by technology also becomes ever more pressing. An increasing range of jobs are already replaced by robotics, computing and artificial intelligence at a seemingly ever-accelerating rate, that threatens to leave huge swathes of populations unemployed and substantially disenfranchised. Estimates suggest that for nations such as the United States, automation could soon replace 50 per cent of all jobs.[31] At the same time new roles are created and new sectors thrive. But there is no guarantee that the people whose jobs disappear will also be able to take advantage of those new opportunities.

Not only is the work that we can each undertake in the world changing, but so too must our core understanding of the world in which we undertake our work. The aspirations we have to support ourselves and our families, the meaning we find in our work, the sense of identity and agency that comes from engaging in productive craft and labour, all increasingly depend on our ability to repurpose our own talents and capabilities and re-define what success means to us. So often, this is not simply a question of re-inventing ourselves as economic agents, but of revising or re-creating our definitions of who we are; and editing or rewriting our stories as human beings. We are in a constant process of becoming; of leaving prior versions of ourselves behind as we adjust to pursue new ends. Without cultivating that capability to come to terms with change, we risk losing the ability to find meaning in our work and even losing our ability to find opportunities for gainful productivity at all.

This is a challenge for us all and we shall need to take collective action to make addressing it more accessible across the mainstream of society. Advantage will accrue to the businesses, governments and non-profit organisations who best equip us to adapt.

Living purpose for a working world

Conventional views on purpose in enterprise focus on purpose as something fixed and pre-determined. The analogy is often used of the North Star. This even carries into views on purpose that prioritise creating a social good. Larry Fink's most recent open letter to CEOs itself refers to a company's purpose as its 'north star' in today's 'tumultuous environment'. Or to give another recent example, Michael O'Leary and Warren Valdamis describe the 'North star of a deeper social purpose' in their inspiring book on accountable capitalism.[32] But while the notion of a North Star captures the idea of purpose as offering a direction to pursue, I'd argue that it has less to tell us about the process of repurposing in changing conditions. The North Star is a glorious beacon, but unlike humans it always appears in the same place. As Walter Benjamin wrote in 1934, 'The rigid, isolated object . . . is of no use whatsoever. It must be inserted into the context of living and social relations'.[33]

When our purpose is no longer itself fit for purpose, if we hold onto it without correcting our course, it can lead us astray, with the apparent self-assured confidence of a sat-nav that is lacking an essential update and which, if we follow it, guides us confidently and reassuringly straight into a freshly dug quarry.

The fixity that was once the virtue of a clear purpose, simplifying complexity and providing the heuristics to make the right path easier to follow, can change from source of advantage to source of failure; unchecked it can lead to ever-greater magnitudes of error. It is interesting that O'Leary and Valdamis conclude their book by invoking the need for 'cathedral thinking', reminding us that work on cathedrals often had to begin a hundred years or more before the building could be completed and suggesting that we must pursue longer-term goals. While their book is compelling and I share many of their views, our shared human future is not a building that can be planned, brick by brick, ahead of time. It is true that we must overcome short-termism, but we must do so without stunting our capacity for ongoing adaptation to a changing world in which further fresh priorities and new opportunities will present themselves over time. The North Star analogy makes us think of the Star of Bethlehem, and it is perhaps unsurprising that it leads to a redemption narrative fit for cathedrals and the promise of eternal salvation. But, of course in human contexts, purpose always remains imperfect and there to be further improved.

We also often think about the absence of purpose as if it is something that our organisations have lacked from the start rather than lost over time. And we tend to think that purpose comes 'authentically' from within ourselves rather than as a product of our relationships with others. The evidence, however, shows that purpose is usually missing not because there was no 'reason why' our organisations were created and developed but because that reason no longer drives an adequate response to the emerging world around us. Purpose is not best found through inward-looking analysis or simply being true to our current selves, but from a perceptive and insightful response to emerging changes in stakeholder needs. Purpose is best not imposed from within as an act of will but inter-created through our increasingly complex relationships. It can determine not only how we marshal our own resources but also how we tap into the far greater forces for change that operate beyond the boundaries of our own organisations.

If we fail to acknowledge that even negative outcomes can usually have been created with initially good intentions, reforming efforts may fall on deaf ears. If we fail to tie new purpose to the creation of breakthrough value, then our efforts will be wasted or of limited impact. And if we fail to overcome the momentum of repeated response cycles of intention, action and effect that no longer work in an environment of changed realities and expectations, then decline is almost certainly inevitable.

The progress trap

Progress traps[34] occur when incumbent activities lose their viability, but only after having gained so much momentum that they can seem almost impossible to escape. It is as if the invisible rules guiding them are an algorithm that has developed a glitch, stopped working for us and started working against us. The use of fossil fuels, for example, has powered our development but in so doing has created a dependence on what we now know to be a deeply destructive form of power.

Because much of what we currently have appears to depend upon our existing norms, they can appear fiendishly difficult to change. Indeed, there is usually a huge resistance to change from vested interests whose short-term objectives may run against the longer-term interests of the majority and ultimately even of themselves.

Progress traps are found at every level of human cooperation and are relevant to all forms of organisational life, from business to non-profits to government. They are also driven by the cognitive biases associated with sunk costs. The prior commitment that we have made to invest in what has become the status quo holds us back from changing direction even when our prosperity and wellbeing objectively require it. We too often fail to let go of our prior expectations.

Opportunity costs

Sins of omission can be even more consequential than sins of commission. We underestimate their impact because we don't even realise what we have failed to achieve.

The costs of failing to repurpose are incalculable. They reside in the business opportunities that we miss out on; the lives that we neglect to change; and the futures that we fail to create.

While the impact of COVID-19 and its variants has been recognised as the biggest economic shock in 300 years, and other shocks such as the pressures that conflict can place on global energy and food can also be assessed and quantified, there quite simply is no way of calculating the full cost of our collective failures adequately to repurpose, as we can't measure what could have been.

But we can note some of the consequences of inaction. A failure to repurpose destroys value for all stakeholders. Failures to repurpose reduce our engagement, impede our productivity, degrade relationships with investors, reduce trust among all parts of society and leave us exposed to the greatest risks, from individual loss to the kinds of 'black sky hazards'[35] that could ultimately pose the greatest dangers to all of humanity.

The differential in outcomes between success and failure in repurposing our organisations is likely to become exponentially greater still in the coming years and decades as the complex threats of our most pressing global challenges multiply the uncertainties that we face and increase the disparity of outcomes that we may be most likely to achieve.

The Purpose Upgrade as a core capability

There is now an urgent and important need for an approach to developing organisational purpose that is as dynamic as the changing world.*

The ability to upgrade our purpose must become a core capability of any enterprise. That capability must enable leaders to address their stakeholders' most pressing needs, to build mutual commitment with the groups that they serve, and to

---

* The absence of such a discipline from business schools around the world is somewhat akin to teaching academic subjects from chemistry to geography to school pupils without ever stopping to teach them more fundamentally how to think.

achieve inclusive outcomes that mobilise support inside and outside the organisation.

A Purpose Upgrade is not about providing fringe benefits but rather about upgrading the central basis of an organisation's success and legitimacy. It represents the single most powerful lever we can pull to re-imagine, re-invigorate or redirect every aspect of the value that it creates.

The very intention to create a Purpose Upgrade can change the cognitive environment of enterprise leadership and creates a space for taking a more strategic and comprehensive approach to formulating purpose at every level across a business.

In Part Two we'll explore a model for repurposing business by solving better problems, enabling collective change and creating more ambitious and inclusive outcomes.

For your enterprise

- When and why was your organisational purpose formed?
- How has the relevance of this purpose changed? Can it lead to negative impacts? Or to missed opportunities? Does it now need to be understood differently or more comprehensively?
- What sunk costs may be impinging too heavily on your decisions? Or what incumbent expectations may now be holding you back?

Part Two

THE MODEL

Chapter Three

A STATE OF EMERGENCE

Choosing which problems to tackle defines the upper limits of our success. A Purpose Upgrade therefore begins by finding better problems to solve.

Conventional approaches to economic and business thinking strip away human context in a reductive focus on pre-defined propositions and transactions. Re-appraising this context can lead to opportunities to address radically more valuable and important needs.

Seeing the world through our stakeholders' eyes helps us to overcome our internal biases, assumptions and limiting perceptions, to find opportunities to make a bigger difference to people's lives and to unlock unprecedented business opportunities as a result.

Five shifts of perspective are identified in this chapter to unlock value. These comprise an expansion of focus to include:

- Whole-person context
- Whole-social context
- Whole-business context
- Whole-community context
- Whole-environmental context

Expanding our focus to integrate these perspectives restores our situational intelligence and opens the door to creating greater change that is better aligned with our stakeholders' needs.

It can drive a form of enterprise that makes a greater contribution to its stakeholders and develops more valuable relationships. And it supports leaders in envisioning a shift from a world of scarcity and fragmentation within existing assumptions to a world of fresh possibility and greater wholeness beyond them.

From problem-solving to problem-finding

Purpose is born as a coping mechanism to address our problems. It is perhaps for this reason that there is a widespread tradition of seeing the virtue of facing our greatest difficulties. Among the most powerful religious symbols of all time, we find the Crucifix as a symbol of redemption through suffering in Christianity, and the Aum symbol in Hinduism that represents Ganesh, the remover of obstacles, clearing the path to spiritual growth. The most admired figures in history are noteworthy for their achievements in overcoming adversity, whether we think of Nelson Mandela's extraordinary resilience and vision in emerging from twenty-seven years in prison to lead a brutally divided South Africa to democracy as its first president, or Abraham Lincoln's accomplishment in bringing political opponents together in leading the United States out of civil war. In business, we talk about understanding a customer's 'pain points', because we know that these are the triggers of their most important decisions and they will open the doors, if not to eternity or historic acclaim, at least to their most significant motivation and budgets!

Once we accept a definition of the problem we are trying to solve, however, fundamental questions disappear from view. While this can be useful in providing a focus, over time it can cause us to overlook most of the fresh opportunities to create value that may be available to us. Just as purpose makes action possible, action makes the need to repurpose inevitable. Solving a better problem can unlock far greater value than finding a new way to solve a previously identified problem.

In almost any organised activity, one of the most powerful ways to create breakthrough success is to read situations differently, re-frame the nature of the challenge addressed and thereby make it possible to set a new course of action that increases the value that everyone involved can create and enjoy. Setting out to find and solve more valuable problems is an especially useful mindset in unpredictable and interconnected environments in which the dynamics of external relationships are constantly creating new priorities and opportunities.

The emergence of everything

We have lived through a state of emergency during the pandemic. But while not every problem is on the scale of COVID, as we saw in Chapter One, we can apprehend them all through the lens of emergence.

Emergence is a charactcristic of what we have come to call complex adaptive systems. Complex systems are different from complicated systems in that they are non-linear and transformative. In complicated mechanisms, such as clockwork, the correct assembly of the right working parts leads to a predictable outcome. If one part is faulty, it can be replaced without changing the end result. And each part itself is not changed by virtue of being included in the assembly.

In a complex system, by contrast, the outcome is transformative because change emerges across the system as a result of the interactions between its constituent parts. Each part changes its own behaviour as a result of this interplay and in so doing influences the behaviour of the others. This creates a new wholeness that cannot be explained by simply adding up the parts. This is one way in which human consciousness transcends Artificial Intelligence.

In simplifying groups of people into aggregates of individuals, as much market research does, conventional economic thinking hides the true determinants of behaviour, leaving us blind to the possibilities for sudden change as new behaviours and norms are adopted across whole groups or even populations. Much research compounds this limitation by operating within the assumptions of the status quo and conventional industry practises. It is therefore much less likely to lead to breakthrough insight.*

If we think of a group as merely the aggregate of its individuals, then by understanding the preferences or intentions of the individuals within the group, or even a representative sample thereof, we believe we can likely predict the actions of the group as a whole. This analysis misses the crucial observation that the most important influences on behaviour emerge from the interactions between members of the group. A change in context that impacts on these influences can therefore lead to rapid shifts in behaviour that defy prior expectations. The larger and more interconnected the group, the greater the scale at which such shifts can occur. Understanding, unlocking

---

* Market research in Russia, for example, has conventionally classified beer as a 'soft drink'. The fact that this may strike us as amusing also shows how limiting economic assumptions can be. For many people, choosing a beer or a cola while watching a football match with friends are fairly likely alternatives.

and working with the interactions and influences across the group can therefore be a powerful source of breakout success. Failing to do so leaves us blinded to the potential for our greatest threats as well as opportunities. The tide of social opinion and choice can turn rapidly and powerfully.

One problem after another

Emergence makes sure that we never run out of problems to solve. This may explain why the founding stories of our favourite enterprises often seem more non-linear and organic than the clear-cut models of conventional approaches to corporate strategy. Entrepreneurs typically start their businesses by stumbling across an unsolved problem and finding a way to solve it. They then grow their ventures by making the most of the opportunities that present themselves as they progress. Start-ups can be among the most purposeful of all businesses because they are closest to a founding problem that they are created to solve, and because purpose is often the currency that they use to engage staff, partners, supporters and even in some cases their first clients and customers, before they even have all the money or other resources in place to deliver on their promises. This also aligns with the frequent success of the 'reluctant innovator',[1] who creates an enterprise not because they want to run a business but because they identify a need to which they feel compelled to respond. Google was started as a class project by Sergey Brin and Larry Page, who simply wanted to search for websites based on their interconnectedness rather than on how many times the search term appeared on their page; it wasn't even a company for thirty-two months.[2] Apple Inc. was launched not with a business plan but with a demo Apple 1 computer and a first order to assemble fifty units.[3] Thomas Edison had created more than 1,000 products before he created General Electric in 1890 to sell his inventions, describing his philosophy in the simple claim: 'I find out what the world needs, then I go ahead and try to invent it.'[4]

The business of context

Most typically, most of the time, business leaders have become accustomed to already knowing what problem they are trying to solve. If you are McDonalds, you are trying to sell more burgers; if you are the Coca-Cola Company, you are trying to sell more soft drinks; if you are Kodak, you are trying to sell more film . . . and of course that itself becomes the problem when the world outside changes, in the latter case of course as it did to move away from film to digital technology.

While clear focus can initially lead to efficiency, over time the blind spots it creates may become pernicious, undermining the basis of our understanding, decisions and actions, at best leaving potential value un-created and at worst actively causing harm. The risk is made worse by conventional economic thinking that de-contextualises decision-making, reducing humans to 'resources', people to 'consumers' and, as we saw previously, misconstruing communities as 'markets'. The core assumption of economics is *ceteris paribus* – all things being equal. But in no human context are all things ever equal. This is especially true in environments of rapid change.

Because we take our cues from the people closest to us, organisational boundaries can therefore further cause us to be better attuned to the assumptions and biases of our peers than of our external stakeholders, causing us to see the challenges within our organisation more clearly than we perceive the far greater change taking place in the lives and work of our customers and other stakeholders outside the business.

This can be exacerbated by the scale of global organisations, in which decisions affecting tens or hundreds of thousands of people can be taken with too little exposure to the lived realities of the people who are affected by these decisions or for whom they are taken. Much of the world's power is exercised through the keyboards of financial analysts who may have little experience of business operations at all.

Wider contextual analysis is further made necessary because in today's environment our problems come so deeply nested and entangled within each other. The problem of the invasion by Putin of Ukraine in February 2022 could not be separated from the problem of inequalities which placed so much wealth and power within the hands of one man, from the problem of energy dependence which meant that so many nations had effectively been funding that inequality through their imports of oil and gas, or from the cost-of-living crisis driven by rising energy prices.

Home economics

The relationship between humans and their context can perhaps most clearly be understood in our notions of 'place'. The relationship between our dwelling, our aspirations and the possibilities available to us has always been tightly reciprocal. A step change in our environment with the advent of agriculture is widely held as the inception of a new era of human development that has profoundly shaped everything that has followed it. Our most ancient structures, such as the prehistoric monument Stonehenge, demonstrate an awareness of our own finitude and a struggle against mortality. Great cathedrals, temples and mosques inspire awe of the divine and readily awaken in our awareness the sensation of being a small part of a greater order. Our environment influences our biology, changes our attitude and conditions our behaviours. Psychologist Peter Ward suggests that the structure of western homes, with their affordance for privacy, territory and a room of one's own, have contributed to a western prioritisation of the individual over the group.

The de-contextualising influence of economic thinking reaches right into the places we inhabit, shaping the environment that structures our perceptions and defining much of what is possible for us in our daily lives. Our built environment bears little resemblance to the settings in which we have evolved, but we are still attracted to the kinds of landscape in which humankind has spent most of its time. Psychologists Stephen and Rachel Kaplan have argued that in modern urban locations, the movements of our eyes are more focused on details and less prone to flit agreeably from one location to another than they are in natural environments. This directed attention increases cognitive strain over time and can be alleviated through exposure to nature. The effortless, involuntary attention of a walk in the woods can help us to release the burden of our current focus, the better to re-appraise what is most important to us and repurpose our actions afresh,[5] letting go to begin again.

The ultimate expression of de-contextualisation may be seen in the kinds of global suburbs where people are so separated from each other that they can rarely venture beyond their own garden on foot. Perhaps the epitome of this can be seen in the new town of Brasília, intended to become the ideal urban environment and which has probably succeeded — if you are a car rather than a person! It was designed with no pavements, no street corners, no opportunities to bump into anyone you know or even don't know, and largely without street names:

addresses are comprised of numerical codes designating spaces on an invisible grid as if to control the city with the ultimate economic algorithm and strip away all human meaning.

The problem is that this form of development creates dangerous fragilities. When things collapse in monoculture urbanity, they really collapse. The beacon of US car-making, Detroit, Michigan, is a salutary warning of what happens when a city becomes the embodiment of an industry that has lost its viability. It went from building nine out of ten of the world's cars to a population explosion and bankruptcy.

The antidote to a de-contextualising form of development is, of course, to re-contextualise, to restore nature, to diversify economic activity, and to bring people back together through the complex patterns of adaptive activity that come naturally to us when our environment enables it. We are at our happiest not only when we are within touching distance of nature, but also when we can stumble across human contact by adventuring out without having to plan for it and when our opportunities are varied enough to keep our minds and bodies fresh.

The fifteen-minute city concept, for example, puts people back at the heart of planning. When we can live, work and play within a fifteen-minute walk or bike ride from home, we restore meaning and connection to our local environment and create a context in which we can thrive. COVID-19 has given many of us a taste of commute-free life and perhaps drawn attention to the things that may currently be missing in the areas in which we live, thereby identifying new opportunities for enterprise to better serve our needs.

What's your problem?

Emergence casts problem-solving in a radically new light that challenges the conventional approaches of enterprise. Understanding problems as emergent phenomena invites a number of useful expansions of focus, including from what we supply to how people use what we supply; from our domain of control to our broader zone of influence; and from our self-interest to the mutual interest that we can share with other stakeholders, including groups whose importance we may have previously overlooked or underestimated.

The Five Contextual Shifts Framework

In business, we may obsess over the minutiae of our own product and service offerings. Often we would do better to pay greater attention to how, why and with whom people are (or indeed are not) using them, and the broader goals of which this usage may be a significant or indeed relatively trivial part.

It can be valuable to expand our attention to focus on our customers in their whole-person context, as opposed to simply our current conception of the nature of our transaction with them. We can further expand our attention to the social or professional environment in which they find themselves; or shift further to the community environment in which we can address their needs; or even the built, natural or planetary environment in which they work and live.

I have identified what I call the Five Contextual Shifts framework to find greater purpose in discovering more significant problems to solve. It can help us to add previously overlooked value to our organisations and, even more importantly, to the people whom we serve.

Whole-person context

When we reduce the people whom we serve to the notion of 'consumers', we represent them as something less than they truly are; as if their sole agency was to diminish by however many units the world's supply of whatever we happen to be selling them. We forget that they are people, doing things that interest them with people they care about more than they care about or are interested in our products and services, and in which context our products and services make a small contribution to a bigger picture. As a result, we can miss out on the best opportunities to understand current and potential customers on their own terms, fail to understand their true goals and priorities, and fail to support them in the journey of change they seek, whether pleasurable or soulful, trivial or of life-changing significance.

To illustrate the point, most mechanical garages that I've been a customer of (and maybe I'm unusually lucky here) have been good at least at the job they believe they are in the business of doing: servicing and maintaining cars. But how good are garages typically at helping us reduce the cost and increase the reliability of motoring by better maintaining our own cars in the first place? How often do they help us get on with daily life by offering to drop us off at home or at the office when we've taken our car in for repair (when, given that we've just handed them our means of transport, we've created quite a logistics headache for ourselves to become their customer in the first place)? When we are back at the garage waiting for them to finish up, how often can we access free Wi-Fi to check emails or watch a quick video while we wait? How hard would it be, after all, to make this available in the waiting area that they need to have anyway?

By reconnecting with the whole-person context of the people we serve, we open the door to a more meaningful relationship with them that unlocks greater reciprocal value. It helps us to overcome the narrow limitations of a consumerist mindset to uncover greater needs. Without this expansion of focus, many businesses fail even to ask themselves if what they are offering is truly useful and beneficial to a customer in the first place. Think food businesses that hook us on a sugar and salt rush but ignore true nutritional needs. Think insurance providers who focus on convenience of purchase but include exemptions in the small print that make their product ineffective at the moment when you are counting on it to help you get back on with your life. Or toy manufacturers that invest in large, brightly coloured packaging and shelf space but provide little educational or other lasting value through playing with the toy. Our customers are almost always the people who can do the most to improve their own lives and outcomes. To create lasting value, we must ask ourselves how we can get better at helping them to do so. This holds the key to longer, more mutually beneficial relationships grounded in the genuine service of meaningful problem-solving.

We can similarly gain from better understanding our other stakeholders as people in context. We can recognise shareholders as investors seeking to exchange commitment for a reward that may be both financial and meaningful; we can see employees as colleagues whose discretionary efforts and talents can be empowered but not commanded; we can appreciate suppliers as partners whose long-term success can be intertwined with our own for mutual benefit; and we can acknowledge members of the public as citizens whose tax-paying, law-abiding, choice-making, peer-influencing and country-shaping behaviour allows our businesses to exist.

These stakeholders all participate in cycles of change that have consequences for our enterprise as well as for themselves. Upgrading these cycles of change through the perception of true need in context is a reciprocal victory. The challenges ahead of us will demand adaptation in our daily habits, practices, work, leisure and in our fundamental understanding of who we are and the world that we live in. Leaning into this change and making it easier for people to embrace holds the key to escaping the limits of current industry norms and creating value that lasts. Brompton bicycles didn't succeed by just promoting their foldable bikes *per se*; rather they succeeded by making it easier for people in cities to get some fresh air and exercise on their commute while causing less pollution and saving money. They achieved this by deliberately focusing on locations where riding their bikes would make the most practical difference to people's lives and by seeding their 'People for Movement' campaign to unclog roads and arteries in one new daily routine. Discovering the underlying problems of all an enterprise's stakeholders makes it easier to set a compelling agenda for shared action that aligns their needs.

Whole-social context

We further gain from understanding our stakeholders in their social context. Even the word 'customer', while substantially less loathsome than 'consumer', leads us to imagine that we serve a single person and that that person is defined through the transaction through which they pay us for a good or service. This partial truth can cause us to overlook the influences over our designated customer's behaviours and decisions, the true benefits they seek to create and the broader picture of which their custom is a part. Our customers are rarely alone in any of this.

When we eat at a restaurant, for example, if we think from the perspective of the individual transaction, waiters likely reduce rather than increase the value that is obtained by the customer. In a buffet-style lunch, you escape the relative tyranny of having to wait until your food is ready; instead, you can take it whenever you are ready (and return again). You escape the portion control of the chef and are free to eat as little or as much as you like. And you are liberated from the constrictions of the menu and free to combine any items you fancy into any series of dishes you choose. In terms of classical economic thinking and satisfaction-maximising behaviour, the buffet *should* beat table service any day.

But the reason restaurants rightly largely eschew buffet service is that we mostly dine out not for the food alone, but rather for the experience of spending valued time enjoying it with each other. Table service is a ritual that highlights that we've chosen to be together, addresses us on equal terms as guests and allows us to share an experience in which our relationship to each other is more important than the ostensible 'utility' of the offering.

It's no coincidence that one instance of catered food that is primarily offered as a buffet is the hotel breakfast: it constitutes one of those times when we frequently do eat by ourselves, preparing for that meeting or getting our thoughts together for the journey home.

The social context applies equally to business-to-business products and services where the primary influence on the decision-maker you seek to influence is most likely to be their relationship with the leader to whom they report. Helping them to work better with their line manager and avoid the risk of a strained relationship can be a more effective lever to pull than increasing the intrinsic quality of a proposition. Genius examples of this include businesses that create bespoke materials to support employees in justifying a purchase to their boss and in tracking the benefits of the investment with them.

People don't want our products and services as much as they want the relationships that they use them to build. They seek to appear intelligent at work, savvy to their friends, thoughtful to their families and attractive to their potential partners. They don't want the jobs we have to offer, but rather they want to build a livelihood that supports them in becoming the person they wish to be, with and through the people whom they care about. Solving better problems comes from expanding our understanding of context to more closely tie into the bigger picture that really counts and better supporting people's aspirations for connection and social standing.

This lever is at its most powerful when just as we shift from people's wants to their underlying needs, we also shift from empowering people to create superficial 'impressions on' to more meaningful 'experiences with' the people whom they care about. The By the Way Bakery founded by Helene Godin with locations in New York and now also Connecticut, has built a thriving old-fashioned bakery producing small batches of hand-made deliciousness by following one apparently simple philosophy. They spotted that on many social occasions someone is unable to enjoy the treats that everyone else gets to choose, because they are gluten-intolerant or have another food allergy or a religious restriction on the ingredients that they can eat. They believe that no-one should be left out of a celebration, so in the spirit of inclusiveness their whole range of baked goods is gluten-free, dairy-free and kosher certified. The valuable togetherness of any group is lost when people are excluded. The essence of true hospitality is to make everyone feel welcome.

What is most important to your customers in their relationships and what useful problems to solve can this reveal? What matters most to other stakeholders outside the enterprise among their peer groups? And what is most important to your colleagues inside the business in the context of their fellow professionals, friends and family?

Whole-business context

Value is often lost by overlooking opportunities for change and innovation that come from working better across the different teams and business units within an individual company. Early in my career I worked in a cosmetics business where the competition that was most feared was the competition from other brands within the same company. A division that led the global market in skincare had no mechanism even for working with another division that had unparalleled access to hair salons just at a time when, in many countries of Europe, the market for skincare products bought in hair salons was taking off. As a result, the business was absent from that market, leaving opportunity needlessly missed. There were also several thousand scientists working in research and development but utterly closed in their mindset to the insights from their marketing teams which indicated that parts of the market were shifting towards more holistic, alternative approaches to health, beauty and wellbeing, because that depended on whole systems of knowledge that lay outside of their particular domain of chemistry. There was more retrenchment and resistance than an active embrace of fresh sources of knowledge.

Even businesses that function well internally and provide what in principle may be a superior option for their end customers can nevertheless fail by overlooking the roles that other businesses also need to play alongside that offering for it to be truly useful. A highly effective treatment for diabetes failed because most prescribing doctors lacked access to the testing equipment needed to know that it was safe for a particular patient. A pioneering approach to run-flat car tyres by Michelin itself fell flat (excuse the pun) because the equipment needed to fit them cost more than it was worth to mechanical garages to have them, as the proportion of their customers needing the run-flats was so low.[6] When as customers we buy into technology the choice is often not just which is the best product but which will be supported by the best systems of service provision, whether it's a phone with access to the apps we most want to use or an electric car with access to convenient, affordable and widely available options for charging.

Value is often lost by overlooking the role of businesses or other organisations with whom we may not even have a direct relationship but on whom our customers depend for the totality of their solution. How many local businesses have suffered because of changes in the free availability of parking without commensurate improvements in public transport? How many restaurants and caterers have closed because major employers of office workers move or close? Our focus on competitiveness within our currently defined boundaries and industry conventions can cause us to overlook the degree to which any business offering is made possible, viable and fruitful through other business and organisational activity in its operating environment. By examining the links that either impede or advance our actions and, even more importantly, the activities of our customers, we can identify previously hidden yet potentially transformational problems to solve and challenges to address, either within our business or through new forms of partnership that enable us to solve bigger problems together than we could otherwise do alone.

Business clusters may also be a widely overlooked, under-researched and valuable source of long-term business success. They comprise a geographic concentration of firms, related businesses, suppliers, service providers and logistical infra-structure in a particular field, such as IT in Silicon Valley, cut flowers in Kenya or diamond-cutting in Surat, India. The city of Amsterdam has chosen to invest in electric vehicles by provid-ing a subsidy that enables taxi drivers serving Schiphol airport to purchase Model S Teslas, sending a strong message to people arriving in the Netherlands about the priorities and expertise of the city. Leading in the sector has meant that EV-related businesses such as Segway and Helios (fast-charging systems for electric buses), EV Box (charging stations), Ebusco (elec-tric buses), GreenFlux (chargers) and Allego (fast chargers) have located in the Dutch capital, creating thousands of jobs and building a wealth of specialist expertise. A similar commit-ment in Hamburg to renewables through city-ownership of the energy utility has led to a cluster of almost 200 firms in wind, solar and biogas. Clusters often also attract support and partic-ipation from local academic institutions and become a defining feature of the locality. In the case of Hamburg, Hamburg Energie has partnered with Siemens Gamesa Renewable Energy and the Institute for Engineering Thermodynamics at Hamburg University of Technology for a Future Energy Solutions project, harnessing thermal energy stored in volcanic rock.[7]

Clusters reduce costs, increase knowledge transfer and empower reciprocal success, creating multiplier effects that enable long-term investment such as better transport links. Larger businesses can lead in the development of clusters by identifying strategic gaps such as a particular skills deficit and addressing them through partnerships with local institutions as well as providing contracts that make a range of contiguous businesses viable, opening the door to further innovation and mutual opportunity.[8] By leaning into society's greatest needs, businesses can align themselves with the opportunity to build more strategic partnerships with a greater body of available allies who share in their understanding of that need.

With so many cross-cutting issues that affect all players in an industry, trade associations and other forms of national or global networks can also play an ever-greater role in empowering collective change. In the humanitarian sector, for example, a new category of service provider, dubbed H2H (Humanitarian to Humanitarian, inspired by the private sector acronym B2B) is rising up through a shared H2H network, not to deliver aid directly but to improve the effectiveness of the aid system, enabling innovation to spread across the sector. Examples include better approaches to cash transfer, better assessment of crisis impacts as they unfold or improved communication with people affected by disaster. Without participation in the right networks and the opportunities that they can open up collectively, there would simply not be enough mutual visibility for most of the pioneering H2H organisations to reach the NGOs and other institutions through whom they can make the biggest impact.

What in the broader business environment holds you or your customers back? What pieces are missing? And what hidden opportunities might this reveal?

Whole-community context

We become the people we are through the influence of not only those most close to us but also through the broader direct and indirect influence of others right across our communities. We slot ourselves into the grooves and patterns of behaviours that we see and that most readily come to mind. This can be a problem if we are lacking in good influences and positive role models. Local Village Network, a non-profit that takes a village mindset to creating positive influences for young adults from disadvantaged areas, has found that simply introducing young people to ten adults in gainful employment transforms their sense of what is possible in life and opens the doors to futures that would otherwise remain invisible and inaccessible to them.

Just as human insight is needed to understand our customer as a whole person in a social context instead of downgrading them to the status of a 'consumer', cultural insight can be harnessed to better understand the often overlooked, invisible or poorly understood cultural forces that have an impact on our lives, perceptions and choices in the first place.

When I was growing up, brands were big news. A new release of Nike trainers was something I'd await with keen anticipation, and just the chance to see them in a shop for the first time could provoke a trip into town. Times have since become perhaps so interesting (remember the apocryphal Chinese curse?)* that brands can no longer claim such intrinsic importance. As the world becomes more interesting, with an ever-greater variety of sources of stimulation vying for our attention and ever more ways to engage with the people we most want to follow, brands risk appearing relatively more

---

* 'May you live in interesting times!'

dull, superficial or even ridiculous. During the invasion of Ukraine, brands pulled advertising that could not live alongside the news, after a backlash that included a reaction against CNN coverage of air strikes being interrupted with an inanely cheerful advert for boneless chicken wings.[9] But while this example is an extreme case, too much contemporary marketing may nevertheless now appear irrelevant or even run counter to our most pressing priorities.

While paying attention to tone and instigating tactical responses to changing circumstances may be needed in the short run, long-term success will come from identifying deeper shifts in the factors that will ultimately drive how we live, work and connect, and finding ways to shape our collective response to them. The best businesses today undertake a form of cultural entrepreneurship that actively supports us in making the most of a changing environment.

Sarah Fulton Vachon, the founder of Citizens of Soil, has told me how she launched the fledgling olive oil brand not just to spread the taste of traditionally made Cretan olive oil to a wider world, but also to restore the capacity of local smallholder artisanal farmers to make a living from their traditional skills, while preserving the quality of Cretan soil from the kind of intense farming for mass markets which strips all vegetation from olive groves and turns the soil dry and barren. What started with the aim of getting a better market rate for a community of farmers led to the creation of the brand and a partnership with the charity Kiss the Ground to support its activities in engaging people in discovering the potential of regenerative approaches to their own farming, stewardship and gardening activities.

The benefits of a focus on community development are especially striking in areas of disadvantage and in developing economies, where change can play a more fundamental role in improving lives and creating whole new markets in the process. Hindustan Unilever, for example, saw that many of India's poor were excluded from the benefits of entrepreneurship and the products of convenient daily hygiene, so decided to engage women in small, under-privileged rural villages with fewer than 2,000 inhabitants to deliver Unilever products directly to people's homes. Project Shakti, as it is known, provides micro-credit and training to the entrepreneurs and already engages more than 45,000 women, serving more than 100,000 villages, fighting the spread of communicable disease and unlocking a whole new business in the process, already worth over 5 per cent of Unilever's total revenue in the country, from communities that are not even reached by advertising.

What changes across society should we most lean into? What problems can we best fundamentally address? And how can we make our activities matter more?

Every business can build a more vibrant, successful and inclusive society in some way, shape or form. Often enterprise leaders can understate the contribution their businesses already make as well as fail to make the contribution and reap the benefits of a more confident and effective approach to changing whole communities for the better. Substantial value can be created simply by identifying ways for communities to collectively participate in the offerings of an enterprise.

Harvard economist Professor Rebecca Henderson is among a growing number of leading voices reminding business leaders to include governance and the rule of law in their consideration of global and local community. She has put it to me that 'there is a huge business case for de-carbonising the world economy because we put the health of the entire economy at risk if we don't, but it is a collective business case, so business has a crucial role to play in re-building our institutions'.

Business cannot succeed where government cannot function, and today's problems threaten to incapacitate governments who cannot solve our problems without the effective engagement and support of the private sector and their citizenry. Businesses can work better with government and civil society partners to create the conditions in which progressive enterprise can thrive. As Rebecca argues, businesses need strong institutions to maintain the society that they serve. Enterprise therefore needs public goods as much as the public does. 'Businesses must protect the institutions that make us rich and free.' Rebecca cites examples of businesses today not only advocating for more stringent regulation of environmental externalities but also engaging with politicians and government at all levels on a whole host of issues such as the protection of minority and civil rights, and playing their part in shoring up rather than undermining the power of democracy and civil society.[10] This is a far cry from the intentions behind much of the 3.4 billion dollars currently spent annually by US businesses on lobbying,[11] which Paul Polman, former CEO of Unilever, has pointedly described as 'legalised corruption'.[12]

What is stopping your customers and those around them from playing the role in their communities to which they would most aspire? What prevents them from engaging with your products and services collectively as a means to fulfil their goals together? What deeper shared motivations today remain unfulfilled and how can collective action enable more ambitious change?

Whole-environmental context

We can unlock tremendous value by reframing the problem of resource use from 'how can we extract the most value from nature?' to exploring how we create greater value *with* nature. This invites us to assess how we can create regenerative cycles that increase resource availability over time. Edzard van der Wyck, co-founder and CEO of Sheep Inc., has told me how he launched the pioneering fashion brand to work with nature not against it. He believes that synthetic materials, micro-plastics and carbon pollution are giving fashion a bad name, and that rather than simply becoming less of a problem, fashion must become part of the solution. That's why he launched a contemporary knitwear brand with a positive impact on the world. Sheep, as he says, 'are heavily involved'. While enjoying a free-roaming life in the high land of New Zealand they not only create the softest Merino wool but in so doing play a part in regenerative farming by keeping their land's soil healthy, closing the nutrient loop and reducing the need for fertilisers. This keeps the wool carbon negative and enables Sheep Inc. to make their claim to be the world's first carbon negative fashion brand. When you buy one of their sweaters, you even get to track the happy life of the sheep who made it and 5 per cent of the profits is donated to regenerative projects working on everything from biodiversity to community development.

Conventional economic thinking leads us to consider the process of supply as linear, in the form of a supply chain. This conveniently but misleadingly leaves out the constraints that can come from diminished access to primary resources over time and the negative externalities of business impacts on society. In the case of the climate emergency this would amount to the largest bill in economic history.

Global business has now reached a scale at which the use of resources can no longer be sustained. Businesses must therefore set aside their linear management models and focus urgently on how to transition instead to a 'circular economy' model, in which resources are no longer simply extracted, but rather in which 'waste' is re-captured and re-used, and materials are designed to be less resource-intensive.

Interflora, the global flowers business, has reimagined its whole operation, with a Purpose Upgrade through which it now seeks to create a regenerative relationship with nature. It is moving towards a zero-waste business model, tackling packaging, pesticides, labour conditions and greenhouse gas emissions across its business and its suppliers. Interflora's gift boxes and ribbons are fully recyclable and Forestry Stewardship Council certified, their cellophane and flower-food sachets are biodegradable and they have cut out the use of balloons and other harmful materials while also electrifying their delivery fleets. This has all come from a deeper analysis of the problems addressed in providing people with beautiful cut flowers in the first place.

While circular economy principles have not reached the ubiquity that is needed, leaving huge potential for pioneers, examples are nevertheless all around us, from Timberland turning tyres into shoes to Johnson Controls creating recycled batteries to Aquazone turning wastewater into fertiliser. Among fast-growth new ventures, British start-up Winnow has developed smart meters that analyse trash to identify what is going to waste. Specialising in commercial kitchen usage, Winnow has reduced food waste and its accompanying loss of profit by half across businesses in over forty countries, effectively preventing one meal from going to waste every seven seconds. Australian company Close the Loop turns old printer cartridges into a blend with asphalt and recycled glass to make a road surface that lasts up to 65 per cent longer than traditional asphalt. These examples all change the nature of the problem that being in each of these lines of business aims to solve.

Considerable progress across businesses all around the world is being made in reducing the use of resources in the supply of goods and services, such as water and plastic, as well as in achieving greater energy efficiency and reducing transportation in delivery. Much further progress remains to be made, however, in better changing models of demand, for example by switching from business models based on customer ownership to subscriptions services or to access on demand. We see well-known examples such as Zipcar for sharing automobiles, but most of the economy has yet to make such a transition. These shifts change the framing of the problem being addressed from people needing a product to people needing access to the benefits that a product can bring about. Ownership is not a requirement of usage.

Many of the best propositions reawaken people's desire to live a life of meaningful action in which they care for one another and enjoy the wonder of access to nature. As Sir Tim Smit, founder of the Eden Project, has put it to me, 'When we wake up and discover how interconnected everything is and that truly we are Earthlings, it changes everything about how we choose to live within the confines of the planet.'

Sometimes the first steps towards greater environmental consciousness may involve looking closer to the workspace. Incorporating features in line with biophilic design, such as exposure to natural light, wood surfaces, the presence of plants and the welcoming of pets into a working environment can already increase comfort and productivity by re-connecting us with nature and restoring our wellbeing. Biophilic design builds on the concept of 'biophilia' developed by the biologist E.O. Wilson[13] to describe our innate instinct to connect with nature and other living beings. It is supported by research that demonstrates significant health-promoting benefits. For example, hospital patients with access to natural views recover quicker and can be discharged sooner, with the potential to save millions in healthcare costs while increasing human welfare.[14]

Businesses that make improvements to the local environment beyond their own facilities can also benefit from the positive impact this can create in corporate reputation, community resilience and in making an area attractive for current and future employees to live and work in. Indeed, businesses all around the world are discovering the benefits of investing in the restoration of local natural systems, working with nature's own dynamics to solve underlying problems and create multidimensional benefits in so doing. For example, Dow has found that restoring a natural wetland can purify water and increase water quality at a tiny fraction of the cost of a built waste-water treatment plant; Allegheny Power rationalises its real estate portfolio, reduces costs and accesses tax credits by evaluating what parcels of land could do for the environment versus what they can do for the company; and Danone invests in local initiatives to sequester carbon, benefit local people and economies, and increase the resilience of local natural systems, as well as enabling other local businesses to invest alongside them to scale the initiative and extend its impact.[15]

What are the most significant environmental impacts of your operations and of the activities of your customers? What addressable challenges are hidden within them?

The context of this book

In my previous book, *Collaborative Advantage*, I discussed the threat of global pandemics, well before the emergence of COVID-19, in a chapter on global problems and how their resolution can be achieved through the right approaches to cooperation and collective mobilisation. I cited the example of Cuba, which has made a speciality of preventing the spread of infectious disease, largely out of a necessity brought about by low healthcare budgets. Remarkably, tiny little Cuba was therefore able to send more volunteer doctors to West Africa to fight Ebola in the early response efforts than any other nation. This not only made a great humanitarian contribution but also opened the door to a new era of diplomatic relations for Cuba, with the Pope advocating on their behalf and the opening of a US Embassy on the island for the first time since the 1960s. One of the key arguments in the chapter was that disasters and emergencies, far from being something that can only happen elsewhere and to others, are something that we are all at risk of and that it is in all our interests to address.

When reflecting on the concept for this book, I sought to draw on some of what I have learned by working with organisations at the front line of humanitarian crises in terms of how purpose is identified and fulfilled in rapidly changing environments where priorities have to be re-assessed. What I did not know as I first pondered these ideas was that I'd be doing some of my early research and drafting during a lockdown in which over 3.9 billion people would be confined to their homes across more than ninety countries or territories, including my own country of residence, the United Kingdom.[16] We shall have to contend not just with the impact of the virus, but with the impact of the response to the virus in more and less obvious ways for many years to come and in a world in which the range of further complex challenges, resource constraints, conflicts and potential existential threats is likely to increase rather than decrease.

Repurposing lives, businesses and government

Fighting COVID-19 depended on our willingness and ability to change our collective behaviour more quickly and radically than many of us will have ever previously experienced.

The first habit to acquire was simply washing our hands more frequently. So far so easy. But within a matter of days the stakes were raised to staying at home under lockdown. For many of us that meant closing our businesses, putting our livelihoods on hold, and potentially losing the very economic engine on which life as normal had depended. And that says nothing of the far greater toll of losing loved ones before their time, in many instances without being able to spend time with relatives and friends during their illnesses, or even coming together to attend their funerals. More sacrifice was asked of us by our civic duty than previously in our lifetimes and arguably never have we given more for our greater good than we did in our collective response.

Even government treasuries had to repurpose on a sixpence at the inception of the crisis, jettisoning hundreds of years of history of collecting taxes to instead finding ways to distribute money to mitigate the impacts of putting many parts of the economy into a form of induced coma. The rationale for this was of course that we needed businesses to survive as we would depend on their value-creating potential to drive our eventual economic recovery.

We have already seen further crises appear to eclipse the pandemic even as its spread in many parts of the world has continued to rise. Subsequent events have also driven purpose-level change. Businesses withdrew from operating in Russia following its invasion of Ukraine; enterprises redirected their activities to support the Ukrainian people; Germany reversed its policy of demilitarisation, Sweden abandoned its long-held neutrality in pledging direct military support for Ukraine and immigration systems have attempted to move from being systems that seek to reduce the inward flow of people to ones that actively seek to accelerate the arrival of refugees. Action has also been required to address a cost-of-living crisis driven by rising energy costs.

The nature of our economic recovery will determine many of our most important future outcomes. There has perhaps never been a time when the quality of our ideas and our capacity to mobilise around them could make a bigger difference. Our long-term success as we pull out of the pandemic and deal with further emergent crises in its wake may require us to repurpose in more substantial ways even than during the spread of the infection itself.

We shall not succeed in this without changing our enterprises and through them bringing change to the world they serve. We cannot achieve this alone, so we shall explore how we can achieve collective change with our stakeholders for the benefit of society and of our businesses next.

For your enterprise

- What emergent factors impinge upon the people we serve? What are their underlying needs now and in the future?
- Who matters to the people who matter to us? How can we help them improve their relationships with each other?
- How can we establish more regenerative relationships with the environment and our communities?

Chapter Four

THE GARDEN OF FORKING PATHS

A Purpose Upgrade sets a new direction for people's work and lives. To 'direct' means to aim people or operations in a particular direction, such as when directing traffic; it also means to guide performance, such as in a play or film. Finding and enabling a new direction combines both journey and story as one.

By identifying shared pathways to mutual success, we can create faster, more sustainable and more easily scalable progress through collective action in pursuing them.

As humans we map our world and plan our journeys in stories. We can therefore use narrative-based techniques to lead more ambitious journeys to positive change, repurposing our capabilities as well as those of our stakeholders. This can include:

- Story-listening: Exploring the stories people use to guide their lives and work.
- Story-finding: Identifying actionable unfulfilled potential for purposeful change in these stories.
- Story-tuning: Aligning stakeholder stories for mutual benefit.
- Story-editing: Empowering improvement in the stories people tell themselves to better drive their own actions.

- **Storytelling: Making promises that pull people towards more purposeful outcomes.**
- **Story-doing: Playing our own part well and earning the trust of the people we serve.**

Understanding and upgrading the patterns of human behaviour encoded in the stories that we use to cope with change is a powerful tool for changing enterprise and the world that it serves.

Changing the story of enterprise

In good creative writing, villains are written not as people who believe themselves to be the 'bad guys', but as people who believe they are the heroes of their own story.

Business leaders are usually not villains, but must now often overcome the shackles of their own prior stories, which may include limiting perceptions about the boundaries of the role that they can best play in their stakeholders' lives, and create new more inclusive narratives of change. Importantly, they must understand that they are not the sole or even primary authors of the future. Enterprise is a part of its stakeholders' stories even more than its stakeholders are a part of its story and it is ultimately the stakeholders of a business who will decide who the 'good guys' are.

On the one hand, business has never been more exposed to criticism, more challenged by threats to its reputation, or more vulnerable at any place in its increasingly complex supply chains. But on the other hand, rarely if ever has the opportunity been greater to succeed by making a bigger difference to people's lives.

Bringing the outside in

The more contextual problem-solving opportunities identified in Chapter Three in turn require a more collective approach to change. The most important narratives in business may therefore no longer be the internal business plan or the tightly controlled marketing message but rather the narratives created and shared across society by people themselves. The most important problems today cannot be tackled by a business operating in isolation. The most interesting businesses are not necessarily the ones paying for mass media ads in the Super Bowl. Rather, they are usually enterprises that engage in meaningful two-way and multi-way dialogue with their stakeholders to achieve collective goals that go beyond anything they could accomplish alone.

Talking to business leaders who are shaping the futures of their cities, tackling systemic problems, or improving communities through meaningful work for the next generation – a common thread to their stories is that they align a more complex set of stakeholder narratives into a shared vision, sewing together complex cooperation for mutual benefit.

We can achieve better outcomes with all our stakeholders by working with their own aspirations and agency. We can achieve this by framing our purpose in meaning that is shared by all our stakeholders; by designing our innovation in ways that allow people to pursue that purpose together; by creating an environment that is conducive to that purpose; and by structuring our partnerships in ways that align the interests of our businesses with the end purpose we empower.

Seeing the enterprise as the enabler of greater processes of change that take place outside the business in the lives and work of our stakeholders opens the door for our enterprise to play a renewed role in the economy and society with a wider range of partnerships and more mutually beneficial relationships with individuals.

Post-VUCA world

In recent years it has become widespread practice to characterise the operating environments of business, government and civil society according to the characteristics identified by the academics Warren Bennis and Burt Nanus and adopted by the US military initially to describe the multi-lateral world following the Cold War. They are expressed in the acronym 'VUCA': volatile, uncertain, complex and ambiguous.

These characteristics leave open the possibility that while difficult to identify, there is nevertheless an underlying reality to uncover in our situational contexts. But is that the full picture?

Social and political commentators have claimed that we now live in a post-truth world. Partly this has been a response to leaders such as Donald Trump and Vladimir Putin. Trump has promoted 'alternative facts' while in Putin's Russia narratives have been ruthlessly controlled and truths suppressed. 'Fake news' has also been blamed on social media, which too often amplifies polarising content regardless of its veracity. Some commentators have even tried to lay the blame for it at the door of French philosopher Jacques Derrida, who developed deconstructionist philosophy and worked away at the foundations of language to reveal contradictions and inconsistencies in the very terms that it gives us through which to apprehend the world. Today, scientists even go so far as to challenge the very notion of an ultimate reality to the situations we confront, as thinkers from other traditions have done throughout history.[1]

It is not, however, the case that truth does not exist *per se*. Indeed, the raw facts of challenges such as the climate emergency are more important to understand than ever before and we must be increasingly diligent in prioritising truth-finding. During the invasion of Ukraine, it became especially important to be able to validate the provenance, date, time and authenticity of video footage. As deepfake technologies improve, even more challenging situations may present themselves. What could be the impact of a truly convincing simulation of the launch of a nuclear strike, for example?

Many of the most important notions of the 'realities' by which we live, however, are not stable and objective. Rather, they are inter-subjective. We actively negotiate them, advocate for them, demonstrate them and emulate them. Greenhouse gas accumulation in the atmosphere is a fact; the degree to which we are capable of responding to this, the changes that are on or off the table and the consequent harm that will further come of it are for now still open questions.

In whichever sector our organisations operate, the most important work of the moment may be to upgrade our shared interpretation of the present through shared understanding that adds value by shaping perceptions, behaviours, actions and outcomes that upgrade life and enhance the conditions needed to support it. This might include introducing new concepts that change people's behaviours, such as the introduction of the idea of a 'designated driver', which normalised the role of someone who might go on a night out with their friends but abstain from drinking, changing the perception of them from the 'boring' one to the 'thoughtful' one.

In a multi-stakeholder environment, new shared understanding can upgrade the map we use to understand each other's actions, make sense *of* the moment as well as *in* the moment and plan for a future that we co-create. For example, many multi-stakeholder partnerships are born of a collective recognition of a need for change and the belief that a greater change can be made possible through shared action, such as when a sector unites in strengthening the sustainable supply of materials that they must all use, often making meaningful changes to the living and working conditions of people supplying those materials and changing the environmental or social impact of their use in doing so.

One present. Infinite possibilities.

The short story 'The Garden of Forking Paths' by Jorge Luis Borges presents the idea of life as an infinite labyrinth structured in time.

It suggests that the fabric of times that approach one another fork, are chosen or neglected, and contain all possibilities, and that each of our choices causes a bifurcation in the options available to us.

It would not be hard to see that level of complexity in the challenges faced by enterprises today. While we are accustomed to planning in a linear way, today's problems often force us to iterate in the light of unexpected events and the actions of people outside the business whom we cannot control and often may not even influence. We are affected by the choices of others as much, if not more than, by our own. We make each other's success possible and our respective failures hard to avoid. What is clear and obvious one day can become problematic the next. What seems impossible to achieve in one moment can rapidly become commonplace.

These trends have, of course, been further revealed and accelerated during a pandemic that the historian Margaret Macmillan has described as a moment when 'the rivers of history change direction'.[2] It is at such moments that the narratives that enhance our agency and invoke the urgency of action can take strongest hold.

The forking paths of transport

I described some of the characteristics of one set of forking paths to a group of senior executives in a construction company along with a group of their key transport clients by drawing on an anecdote from my early childhood.

In an annual ritual my father used to take me to the air show at nearby RAF Halton. The highlight of the show was always the Red Arrows, and for me the highlight of their display would always be the moment when the 'synchro pair', 'Red Six' and 'Red Seven' would separate from the formation and split to opposite ends of the sky to begin what are called their 'opposition manoeuvres'. Most spectacularly, this includes the moment when the pair appear to fly straight towards each other, with a closing ground speed of around 700 miles per hour, as if they are going to collide, but at the last moment turn on their axes to lift their wings out of each other's way and pass within a few feet of each other flying 'belly to belly' on their sides.

When we drive in two-way traffic, we may not have the closing speed of the Red Arrows as we approach oncoming vehicles, but we do frequently have a closing speed of effectively the same level of ultimate danger: sufficient to end our lives in the case of collision. And, like the Red Arrows, we often pass within just a few feet of these oncoming vehicles. But, unlike the Red Arrows, we rarely know who the other driver is; we are not in radio contact with them; we do not train with them on multiple sorties per day; and, with rare exceptions, we are not among the most talented drivers in the world. We know very little about our fellow road-users, their states of mind, degrees of spatial awareness, or disposition towards us. Driving, or using the roads in any capacity, may therefore be one of the most ambitious acts of cooperation we could think of engaging in. The fact that we can do so without even the need for reflection is made possible by a whole ecosystem of norms, rules and codes of behaviour, governing the different roles played by different actors in everything from maintaining the surface integrity of the roads to teaching us how to pass our driving tests.

As the systems we depend upon become subjected to ever-increasing demands, often without proportionate increases in available resources, we may have to find radically new ways to make the acts of cooperation on which we depend work harder for us. This matters right now because in any direction we face, our range of possible futures appear to be spectacularly divergent.

In the case of the roads, we don't really know if we are heading towards a sort of digital, sustainable utopia of transport, with flying taxis collecting us alongside anyone else who happens to be heading in the same direction as us. Or on the other hand, in the light of diminishing resources, whether our future may become a driving dystopia with gridlock on the roads as local authorities struggle to build new capacity or even maintain existing capacity, or in which people will be scared to use autonomous vehicles because their on-board computers risk being hacked by terrorists.

Even if we don't buy into the extremities of either of these scenarios, the fact remains that experts cannot even predict whether driving from London to Birmingham will take more time in ten years from now or less time than it does today. And every change in our systems opens the door to its own fresh challenges. Driverless cars, for example, will be programmed to avoid collision with pedestrians: does this mean we'll need to take action to prevent the more mischievous-minded from using any part of any road as if it were a zebra crossing knowing that there is no chance of being hit? And if there is an accident, who becomes responsible for it?

The important thing to note is that we'll construct our pathway to the future together through acts of cooperation at many levels. The greatest outcomes will be created by those who shape our collective pathways to create change in positive ways and upgrade the systems we depend upon. It is not within the gift even of the businesses or government actors that I was addressing to determine this future. But they do have important roles to play in negotiating it and will have to repurpose their own activities to flex around emergent change, determining and re-determining their own direction and the direction they seek to enrol others in pursuing as they go, often creating visions and plans that of necessity involve other actors, frequently even including those who they might regard as competitors.

This greatly expands our potential for leadership. As Peter Seymour, Vice-President of Marketing and Strategy for Europe at Mondelēz, puts it: 'We need to repurpose strategy to focus on better enabling all our stakeholders to transition from short term wants to longer term needs.' Or as Rebecca Henderson says to me, 'We need to move from "me now" thinking to "we later" thinking and that means changing cultural narratives.' If this sounds like too great a stretch, Ian Goldin reminds me that '20% of actors can achieve 80% of change'. We can begin with the people and partners most aligned with our goals.

The Six Narrative Drivers Framework

Stories represent the most powerful tool for change available to humankind. These are not to be understood as just the fully formed stories that we read and write, but the broader world of observations, memories, hopes, intuitions, perspectives and inclinations present tacitly or explicitly in our inner representations and in our communication with others. Studies have shown that given the choice, we would even rather have a good life-story than a good life.[3]

We saw in Chapter One that stories provide the primary mechanism that we use to cope with the problems that we face, and that this is even true of the most extreme problems such as disasters and emergencies. History shows that the direct impacts of most such catastrophes are small relative to the cumulative impact of the stories that guide us in how we interpret, prepare for, mitigate, respond to and recover from them.[4]

During the invasion of Ukraine, President Zelensky demonstrated not only his remarkable courage but also his capacity for mobilisation through narrative. Before getting into politics, he had played the role of a comedian who became president in a popular television show. And then in a case of life imitating art, he went on himself to become a comedian turned president. The party that he led even adopted the same name as the one in the show: 'Servant of the People'. He retained many of the people who had worked with him on the show as his close advisors, including his scriptwriter who became his speechwriter. He made a moving and powerful case for support for Ukraine, addressing many of the world's parliaments by videolink in a global virtual tour, making it even more personal by relating the story of the invasion to episodes in the histories of each nation that he addressed. He also addressed other less conventional groups, including TikTokers, as people whose own influence, he urged them to understand, could also help to end the war.

Stories guide our most significant decision-making processes. As my friend General Mark Raschke tells me from his former experience guiding senior leaders in the Pentagon and the White House, just as we are unlikely to choose a spouse based on a spreadsheet assessing their various merits in quantifiable terms, society's most senior leaders take their most complex and important decisions with an awareness of data but most significantly with a narrative that they use to make sense of the situation and the action for which it calls.

It is little surprise therefore that the stories that guide us represent the most powerful driver of enterprise and the business environment. Indeed, Nobel prize-winning economist Robert J. Shiller has dedicated his career to demonstrating how shared narratives, so often ignored by economists as unscientific or anecdotal, are the true shapers of economic events. He has built a substantial evidence base, decade after decade, to reveal how economic events reflect the stories we are telling ourselves across society more than any other influence.[5]

Since we are utterly dependent on each other even in our attempts to define ourselves, our narratives must be collective if they are to help us chart a path to better human futures. There is very little meaning that we can truly create alone: the original meaning of common sense is a mutual understanding. However, while we often hear of the value of storytelling in business, the conventional business plan is typically a very unengaging story, because it is usually so narrow and self-directed in scope. But what could it look like if a business plan was so inspiring that people would choose to read it if they didn't have to, and that customers would actively root for the success of the enterprise? Or if partners could use it to better direct the support they offer? Instead of aiming to be the best company *in* the world in your sector, why not aim to become the best company in your industry *for* the world and explore the opportunities for a whole new narrative that this brings with it?

The following narrative techniques that comprise the framework can support us in creating narrative maps to inspire and enable collective action.

Story-listening

True listening doesn't begin by asking people what they think of us in questionnaires or focus groups. Nor does it end simply by accumulating mass data on the decisions people have taken or actions they have performed previously. This information may be useful, but it is insufficient because it is backward-looking and because people usually lack the introspection to understand all their own motivations as well as a vision of all the available possibilities. Too often the questions asked already have our own pre-conceptions baked into their assumptions. Working uncritically with such data risks reinforcing existing limiting biases.

True listening best begins by taking an interest in the lives and priorities of the people we serve in their own terms. It seeks to understand how they represent their own stories to themselves and each other.[6] To do this it helps to step completely outside our own assumptions and agendas to put ourselves in an independent mind space with the sole objective of understanding. What do the people we care about think and say when we are not in the room? How can we best understand them as they understand themselves and each other? Or even in ways that may escape their own notice? What may be their motivations and drivers? What in their underlying situation have they yet to adapt to? And what is holding them back from greater success or fulfilment?

The most empathic organisations and leaders access a treasure trove of knowledge that is too often hidden to the rest of us. This can be the most valuable intelligence of all because it creates a new foundation for change of greater significance to the people we serve. Though often out of sight, it is accessible to us when a customer tells us why they need something. It is accessible when we quietly observe the culture around us. It is accessible when we invite people to talk to us without imposing our own pre-determined priorities. And it is accessible to us when we seek to delve beneath emerging trends to understand the true human dynamics that shape them. We tend to believe we are better at listening than we are, because we rarely find out what we miss. What happens when we actively decide to pay deeper attention to people as if we are an impartial witness, beginning with no knowledge of them at all and allowing their every move to capture our attention? Rarely has there been a more compelling time in which to contemplate the lived experience and coping narratives of the people we serve and who affect our enterprise. It is only through true understanding and empathy that we can unpick the assumptions and limiting perceptions that may be holding people back from embracing a better future.

Alex Edmans has described to me how when the NHS reviewed its constitution through internal discussions, it placed the emphasis on helping people recover from illness. But, after consulting with external stakeholders including patients themselves, they realised that it was just as important to reflect that even when recovery is not possible or lives cannot be saved they still have an immense role to play in alleviating suffering and supporting people as they come to terms with their diagnoses or ultimately reach the end of their lives.

Story-listening involves digging deeper than the specific transactional context in which market research usually operates and that fosters out-dated consumerism and a surrender to historic industry norms and conventions. We may seek to understand more of our stakeholder's world views and develop empathy for their biological, ecological, psychological, economic, and sociological selves. As my friend and green marketing expert John Grant put it to me, we should look for the real cultural power sources and make sure that our starting point is about understanding and benefiting humanity, not just our businesses. The point was further reinforced in my mind by listening to Peter Seymour telling me how he found his way to rediscovering purpose for the Cadbury's brand: he visited a Friends Meeting House and learned more about the Quaker values and beliefs that had been shared by the Cadbury brothers who founded the chocolate business in the spirit of generosity in order to build better livelihoods for workers and a fairer society.

Story-finding

As Feike Sijbesma, Honorary Chair and former CEO of Royal DSM, has told me, 'You learn mostly by listening, reading, observing and traveling. Many leaders are forced to constantly be on stage, presenting and chairing and sending out messages, but real insight comes more from processing the messages you receive.'

Listening deeply to our stakeholders' own stories in their own terms opens the doors to an active exploration of these stories with the aim of working out what we can learn from these narratives and what role we may be able to play in help-ing our stakeholders to better achieve their priorities. Listening alone is a first step, but is not enough by itself. The value of listening increases when we then actively explore our stake-holder's perspectives in a way that is designed to promote the discovery of actionable insight. We can look for surprising connections, anomalies and patterns, and identify the non-obvious truths at the heart of these narratives that can best form the basis for significant positive change. Story-listening helps us to understand the narratives stakeholders use to map their world. Probing those stories further to reveal what lies behind them or limits them can lead to valuable insight that enables us to identify the potential for new maps that offer a path to greater success.

Story-finding goes beyond empathy in finding previously hidden opportunities for us to make a difference. How can we cooperate within our stakeholder's narratives and enhance their own place in them? How can we help them make their own world a better place for them to belong in? What are the differences that can make the most difference to them and how can we bring these about?

The great news for business is that this can often deliver a return on investment that is utterly disproportionate to the cost. Sometimes a small adjustment means everything. When a small independent florist in London called Bloom and Wild decided to offer customers the chance of opting out of Mother's Day communications if they risked being saddened by them, it resulted in thousands of emails of appreciation and extensive media coverage which further inspired the company to initiate the 'Thoughtful Marketing Movement' to spread empathic practice across like-minded brands and businesses. A lifetime of loyalty may be won in an instant of empathy through the kind of human response that shows that your people care and that your enterprise is not just run like a machine. Bloom and Wild further demonstrated its commitment to caring with cut-out newspaper ads this year with bouquets of flowers for children to cut out and colour in for their mothers, 'dad-mums', or anyone who finds Mother's Day hard, as part of their #carewildly campaign. These ads are not about driving sales directly but about building comfort and connection and in so doing becoming a more meaningful part of people's lives.

This analysis opens the doors to better working with our stakeholders' world views, providing the means to re-align their actions and outcomes with these views through the support that we provide.

Story-tuning

The greatest advantage comes from better understanding the needs of all the groups on whom our success depends and finding the right ways to align our interests so that we are acting for reciprocal benefit.

In today's operating environment, stakeholder narratives can easily jar with each other if we are not careful to take them all into account.

Dimitri de Vreeze, co-CEO of Royal DSM, admitted to me an error he made in which he used a presentation created for investors to describe future plans to employees who were left cold by the numbers presented without reference to the purpose and meaning of the new direction. He has since ensured that DSM has always crafted its vision in holistic terms intended to resonate with all stakeholders.

If we run a cancer charity, we may believe that the message that will most motivate donors is to confront them with the terrifying ordeal that facing cancer can be. But that is the last narrative we would want our beneficiaries to hear: we would want to reassure people affected by cancer and their loved ones that there is a lot that can be done to make a recovery, to extend life or to improve the quality of life that remains. The powerful proposition that 'No one should face cancer alone' squared this circle and served to unite stakeholders behind Macmillan's mission for years.

I've also spoken to business leaders whose views were fundamentally changed by engaging with activists protesting against the activities of their brands. Such dialogue can overcome opposition by revealing a more complete picture of the impacts of different decisions and open the door to new possibilities for collaboration and value creation. The turnaround of the Kenco brand to engage in a multi-year journey to sustainable farming in partnership with the Rainforest Alliance was initially sparked by a protest that involved Oxfam in parking their donkeys in front of Kenco's offices to draw attention to the need for better practices in their supply chain. Jerome Foster had previously protested outside the White House for one hundred days to demand greater action on the climate emergency before being given the chance to effect change from within as the youngest member of the White House environment Justice Advisory Council.

As we make the shift to more inclusive and sustainable living, our success will increasingly depend on Purpose Upgrades that we can participate in collectively. We cannot create new life-styles as separate individuals. And businesses too need to work together to provide the environment in which greater transformation can take place. The key driver of success resides in the capacity to pull together the meta-narratives and mutual agreements that empower all actors to find their own role to play.

We can see examples of this in approaches to bringing a Purpose Upgrade to entire districts, such as the repurposing of London's King's Cross as the most sustainable redevelopment project in the UK; in Vauban, where the City of Freiburg in Germany has repurposed a hundred-hectare abandoned military base as an eco-neighbourhood attracting thousands of visitors a year keen to learn how to apply its principles to their own cities; or in the city of Malmö at the southernmost tip of Sweden, where a disused shipbuilding area known as Western Harbour has been repurposed as a mixed-use eco-neighbourhood integrating all of the city's sustainability goals, including building efficiency, renewable energy adoption, green stormwater management, plenty of green space, bike paths and biogas-fuelled buses.

Such approaches help stakeholders to overcome 'chicken and egg' problems, such as when people are reluctant to buy electric cars until there is good provision for charging, manufacturers won't prioritise electric vehicles until enough people want them and enterprise is hesitant to invest in providing charging infrastructure until there are sufficient cars to charge. The solution must come from mutual commitment through negotiations that reach across the private sector, public sector and civil society and that align interests around common purpose and a shared vision.

If we brought everyone that we needed together into one room and asked them all to tell the stories of the positive change they would each most like to enjoy, how could their interests be best aligned? How can we all understand our own actions in terms of the fuller set of benefits that others can use them to enjoy?

Story-editing

The most powerful changes come not from the stories we tell others but from the stories that we each tell ourselves. As renowned social psychologist Timothy D. Wilson has put it to me, 'Each of us needs to make sense of the world and our place in it. And we do so by developing stories about ourselves, who we are, why we do what we do, how we fit into the world around us. And the nature of these stories is critical for our wellbeing and how much we can accomplish our goals.' These more intimate stories define our world view and determine as a consequence the choices that become available for us to make and the criteria by which they are made. The greatest influence we can have therefore is to enable people to change their own stories for the better, opening the door to self-directed change that persists over time.

Timothy has talked me through how story-editing interventions can be used to tackle all sorts of issues, from enhancing people's wellbeing to making us better parents, preventing teenage pregnancies, reducing violence, overcoming prejudice or closing achievement gaps.[7] In fact, they can be used to help us address problems of any nature or scope in any social or commercial context. As we saw previously, every observation contains an interpretation embedded within it. Helping people to perceive a problem or challenge through a frame of reference that changes their own capacity to respond to it is one of the most valuable things we can do. In *Collaborative Advantage* I showed how the concept of 'Good Grief' developed by a death-awareness charity in the UK has been used to help young people see bereavement not as something that you are helpless to address and that affects you only when the time comes but rather as something you can prepare for in advance and take action to heal.

Timothy gives a particularly interesting example of how giving school pupils access to information indicating that pupils who struggle with a subject to begin with usually end up performing well increases pupils' own capacity to handle initial setbacks, because they come to believe that they are following a normal pattern that will reward them in the longer run. The maladaptive pathway of a self-defeating downwards spiral ('I failed, therefore I'm no good at this, therefore I may as well give up') is replaced by an adaptive pathway of self-enhancing narrative in an upwards spiral ('I'm one of those who can do well, the effort will be worth it, so I'll try harder'). The management consultancy firm McKinsey harnessed such an insight when changing the story of people who could not access further promotion from one of failing to advance within McKinsey, leaving and resenting their former employer, to one of graduating to become part of a valuable global network of McKinsey alumni leading change in businesses around the world. This opened the doors to an ongoing relationship with former employees in their subsequent roles for mutual benefit, adding to the prestige and income of both the enterprise and its former colleagues/future clients.

We play into people's self-perception and their aspirations in surprising ways, whether or not we realise it. Public transport is a costly investment by government and oftentimes officials want to send a message that they are frugal with taxpayers' money. Planner Jeffrey Tumlin has claimed that administrators of North American bus and subway services typically choose the most utilitarian-looking materials available for bus interiors and stations, even when more attractive options are no more expensive, just to avoid the *appearance* of wasting money.[8] The resulting buses and stations end up as a result with all the charm of prison toilets and the approach backfires by inducing

134

a sense among users of those systems that they must be poor and unsuccessful to depend on them in the first place. This is exactly the wrong message to send at a time when a climate emergency requires us to shift to collective modes of transport. The commute can be a daily ritual that drives our sense of our place in the world and who we are. Indeed, behind the success of the shift in major cities around the world to Bus Rapid Transit schemes (buses that operate in their own lanes and board like trains at raised platforms, usually with roadside digital displays of timetables) is that the aspirational design of these systems overcomes the 'loser cruiser' image of students who would rather be driving if they could, commuters who can't afford cars or the elderly who can no longer drive. Bus Rapid Transit systems are attractive, cool, and have now taken off in over 150 cities around the world as a smarter way to travel.[9] As Timothy Wilson has further explained to me, 'Humans are innately finely tuned to picking up cues in their environment and creating their inner sense of what those cues mean for them, the kind of person they are and the kind of people that they fit in with.' To ignore or to misuse these cues is to fail to help people further become the people they most want to be and to miss out on the opportunity to support them in addressing their underlying needs.

Storytelling

We are accustomed to hearing that 'seeing is believing'; in reality it may be more revealing to say that 'believing is seeing'. The process of perception is influenced by the meta-stories that define the conceptual landscape through which we perceive the world around us in the first place. Laurent Binet's novel *The Seventh Function of Language* reimagines the death of the literary critic and cultural commentator Roland Barthes as murder in a conspiracy to subvert a truth he had just discovered and was about to reveal: that language has the power to create reality. This premise is not as far-fetched as it may sound. It is well known, for example, that Russians perceive a more nuanced set of shades of red because the Russian language divides the colour into different variations that require distinction. Research also shows that it is easier for us to feel an emotion once we have a word to describe it. [10]

Sir Tim Smit, the founder of the Eden Project, has shared his take with me on the 'Tinkerbell effect' of storytelling. Tinkerbell is a character in Peter Pan who only exists if you believe in her. Tim took the team behind the Eden Project from an idea to the full realisation of one of the greatest adventures of all time in reimagining the relationship between humans and our environment, through the power of stories that he could help enough people to believe with sufficient conviction to make them possible.

Our stories can bring 'reality' into being. We therefore have a great responsibility to choose which stories we tell and share as well as when and how to upgrade to better ones. As Seth Godin, one of the greatest marketers and perhaps one of the greatest storytellers of all time, has put it to me, 'We never know the truth of anything directly. What we know is the story that we receive [. . .] and marketing is the art of telling a story that you are proud to make true on behalf of someone who's willing to engage with you.'

Our best stories embolden and enable our responses to the challenges we face. If we don't tell our stories, we fall short of the contribution that we can make to the lives of the people we serve and care about. It is our responsibility to dramatise the present moment to empower a beneficial journey: whether from risk to security; exposure to comfort; isolation to belonging; or from doubt to confidence. We frame our stories in the form of a garden of forking paths that maximises the benefits of action in relation to inaction, creating urgency and offering agency. It is through our storytelling that we support others in becoming the better version of themselves they most seek to be, among peers whom they care about, in communities that help them to flourish and in an environment that can support their needs.

Because storytelling is at its most powerful when it serves to empower others who make the message their own, the best storytelling does not necessarily require a substantial budget. Greta Thunberg displayed more marketing prowess in her School Strike for Climate campaign and subsequent activism than any chief marketing officer of a global corporation that I have ever met. Her ability to tell the truth and to speak straightforwardly from first principles has made her one of the most effective agents of change of recent history. Her phrase 'How dare you?' from her address to the 2019 UN Climate Action Summit became a driving cultural meme on the most pressing issue of our times.

Story-doing

Enterprises belie their purpose and lose the trust of their stakeholders when their actions do not conform to their stated intentions.

In his comedy news show *The Mash Report,* Nish Kumar memorably savaged the values of the disgraced and defunct construction and managed facilities company Carillion.[11]

He described how Carillion grew by deliberately underbidding on public sector contracts at unsustainably low rates to win tenders, took payments upfront on those contracts and then used that payment to pay off suppliers from prior contracts. This of course is a deeply unethical approach which prices out honest businesses and stores up an inevitable collapse and waste of public money. And it reveals that the true aims of the company's directors were at odds with the purpose stated in their corporate communications.

As Nish said,

> We should have seen it coming. We went on their website yesterday and found a diagram of 'values petals' under a section called 'Our Values'. What is this?! No wonder they've gone under. You can't solve a company's problems by shouting, 'For God's sake, just look at the value petals!' They've spent all the last week screaming 'Oh, magic business flower! Why has thou forsaken us?'

The comedian concluded with an alternative, perhaps more accurate purpose statement for the business. 'I think it's fair to say we can now update Carillion's value flower with this: "We bid, we can't count, we failed, you're fucked!"'

People have every reason to mistrust the stories told by businesses for the self-evident reason that they are biased to influence outcomes that are desirable to the teller. We must therefore not just tell our stories but also commit to enacting them. How can we best live up to our own stories in practice? What actions can we take that are so clear that if someone else told the story of them it would resemble the story we wish to tell?

Trust is earned by behaving in a way that is predictable to our stakeholders because it is based on the story that they have about us. This means using our story as an organising principle around which to innovate and as a criterion for decision-making. It also means not demonstrating behaviour or taking actions that conflict with our story in a way that undermines it.

As Seth Godin further explains to me, 'If you do enough mission action, the mission statement gets made by itself.' A great test of our story-doing capabilities is to ask ourselves if people observing our behaviour would be able to reverse engineer our marketing messages, or at least something consistent with them, for themselves.

John Grant further cites his experience of being asked by Anders Dahlvig, the global CEO of IKEA in 2001, to develop a strategy to communicate for the first time the results of the twelve years of work they had so far put into their environmental sustainability and ethical commitments. After thinking about it extensively, he surprised IKEA's leadership team with a simple one-word presentation: 'DON'T!'. IKEA followed his advice and for years further developed their sustainability credentials before including them in any of their external communications. And it worked. IKEA went on to out-rank General Electric as one of the greenest brands in the US after GE had spent 90 million dollars communicating their commitment to 'Eco-magination'. It has also been rated the most trustworthy institution in Sweden.

Fostering a wholeness of vision

Today's problems pose challenges that cannot be resolved by conventional business planning. We cannot assume a linearity of steps in which we can determine the results through a logical sequence of internal actions. Rather, the ideal action to take depends at all times on a radically reflexive reciprocal relationship between our enterprise and the environment of actors in which it operates.

Our aim must therefore be to increase the probability of success even when we can't define in advance exactly what that success will be. We take action to increase the odds of something positive happening that allows us to build a new adaptive cycle of positive change, correcting and upgrading our actions as we go. In serving society's evolving needs, we better understand the problems that people face and put ourselves in a better place to unlock sustainable value through that better understanding. We form purpose in order to reform purpose again in the light of further emergent change.

Finding your positive deviants

A development initiative in Vietnam was instigated to improve nutrition for the children of poor families in coastal communities. Instead of supplying food aid or going in with pre-existing advice, researchers sought to identify mothers of young children affected by poverty whose health outcomes were unusually positive, or displayed 'positive deviance' in the language of statistics, and to understand what these mothers were doing differently that other mothers might be encouraged to emulate. It turned out that the biggest difference in the behaviour of these mothers was that they had turned to collecting crabs and shrimp from the beach, where they were available for free and in abundance, and adding them to their children's food. These had been considered a poor source of nutrition in the local communities and were actively discouraged by local custom. But the discovery of the unusually high health of children who ate the free seafood enabled researchers to repurpose development efforts to spread new social norms across Vietnamese communities, empowering mothers to nurture healthier children through their own resources rather than by creating dependencies on food aid that could at any point be stopped.

Seeking out the positive deviants among any stakeholder group can help us to identify new roles to play. Understanding what makes particular employees more productive; makes certain customers more loyal; makes specific partners more effective; or even makes some of our own initiatives more successful than others can all reveal unexpected opportunities to replicate and accelerate positive change.

Superconducting change

Once we accept the premise that our stakeholders collectively have more creative intelligence than we do, we can find new roles not only in identifying changes that make a difference but also in designing our offerings to better conduct that change from peer to peer. As Seth Godin has told me, we need to give up the marketing funnel of trying to reach as many people as possible and instead turn that funnel on its side and turn it metaphorically into a loudspeaker, putting it in the hands of the people who most like what we do so that they can reach and influence their peers on our behalf. Joan Fitzgerald, Professor of Urban and Public Policy at Northeastern University and a global thought-leader in the role cities can play in fostering a climate-compatible future, built on Seth's observation with the example of a district-wide initiative to induce greater eco-efficiency in building management in North Carolina, called Envision Charlotte.[12] It was found that key to a successful change in behaviours was to identify a single 'climate champion' for each building, which resulted in a near total participation by 20,000 occupants across the project in voluntary change, including turning down thermostats, powering down computers and other actions to conserve energy.

Unlocking change at scale comes best from creating propositions that our stakeholders seek to share with others because the act of doing so improves their own experience through what are known as 'network effects'. The classic example of this is the fax machine, because there was never any point in owning one unless the businesses with whom you communicate owned one as well. This of course explains why social media networks and services such as Uber or JustPark require a critical mass to work. But it also highlights the opportunities to repurpose around processes of value creation that come either from amplifying positive change or even from dampening negative change in the external environment. Our business plan becomes less a finished guide to internal action and more a starting point of intentions to co-create a shared future.

Changing course as an intentional capability

None of our decisions is ever *completely* right. As Lynda Applegate, Baker Foundation Professor at Harvard Business School and former member of the US Presidential Economic Advisory Council, tells me, 'The only thing I know about every business plan that crosses my desk is that it is wrong: the real question in each case is always "What is the magnitude of wrong?"'

Most business plans, like so many stories in western traditions, follow a pattern of redemption. Today a problem is identified that separates us from the Promised Land. But by undertaking the action proposed that separation can be overcome. The projected ending of these narratives, like so many stories told to children, is to live 'happily ever after'. But in many ways the lessons of emergence may more closely resemble the endings of stories told by so many children: 'and then I woke up and discovered it was all just a dream'. As each adventure closes, it opens the door to the next story.

The end is an illusion because the emergence of change always continues. As we have seen, even a challenge such as COVID-19 and its variants can be best understood in the long run as a harbinger of further things to come. Long-term planning must be more about leaning into the present moment in the light of its lifetime opportunity, value and potential consequence than it is about lunging for a fixed end point that cannot be grasped. Congruence in our narratives becomes more important than consistency.

We entertain multiple possible futures and allow the right one to reveal itself, redirecting ourselves and each other as we go. If every decision we make is in essence a choice to move towards something or away from something, in so doing it re-situates us and puts us in a position to make new discoveries to enable us to further choose our path to better 'correct' the emergent gaps between our state and our original purpose or a newly upgraded purpose. Once again, purpose makes action possible. Action makes the need to repurpose inevitable.

Purpose focuses our environmental scanning, gives a framework for decision-making, and a culture in which individuals come together to make mutually supportive contributions towards the same end. But to prevail over time we also need all of these capabilities along with enough space to question established processes and identify and nurture radical alternatives. Depending on the context, these alternatives may complement existing activity or effectively make it redundant.

One purpose among many

As our world becomes ever more interconnected, interdependent and contiguous, our options are increasingly influenced, shaped and determined by others.

This requires us to situate the story of our own purpose in the broader context of other stakeholder aspirations in play. It is by channelling the most effective change-creating synergy of human purposes that the greatest value can be created.

This brings us to the next topic of our unfolding journey: how to achieve more ambitious outcomes through greater inclusiveness in our goals.

For your enterprise

- How can we make positive change more accessible and attractive to everyone who is needed for it to be achieved?
- Which narratives can empower the greatest progress?
  - What stories are our stakeholders telling themselves?
  - What hidden but actionable truths do these stories reveal?
  - How can we help them change these stories for the better?
  - How can we align and re-align the interests of all the stakeholders we serve?
  - How can we cultivate trust in guiding their path?
- What most value-creating new direction can this enable us to pursue with all our stakeholders?

Chapter Five

THE WEALTH OF CHANGE

In *The Wealth of Nations,* Adam Smith showed how self-interest can lead to a greater good as a by-product. A higher level of success, however, has now been shown to come from putting a greater good first and deriving self-directed benefits as the by-product.

The Wealth of Change comprises the total contribution that an enterprise makes to the world through the change that it empowers its stakeholders to create.

The Wealth of Change can include the creation of five 'Stakeholder Dividends'. These include a:

- Customer Dividend
- Employee Dividend
- Partner Dividend
- Community Dividend
- Planetary Dividend

Each of these dividends not only provides a benefit for the stakeholders of a business, but in so doing benefits the business as well in mutual reward. Each Stakeholder Dividend therefore also serves to create a Shareholder Dividend, both in the literal sense of unlocking a distributed profit per-share and in the metaphorical sense of growing overall enterprise value and achieving broader shareholder objectives.

While we can gain tremendous advantage from uniting the people within an organisation behind a common goal, we can achieve even greater results by uniting with all our relevant stakeholders outside the organisation in shared purpose as well.

The power and peril of measurement

Targets, measures and metrics are powerful tools that can amplify the effects of our actions by helping us to align them to create cumulative change in a particular direction. This may explain much of how we become specialised in particular domains of activity.

During the lockdown phases of the pandemic, like so many others I took to the trails to run during my one outing a day of outdoor exercise. The body likes variety in fitness as much as in nutrition, and one downside of running is that the impact on the joints is focused, repetitive and relentless. Long-distance running could be thought of as the exercise equivalent to eating only one food source all day long, such as an endless diet of white rice. After several thousand steps, the last thing the body needs its next moment of exercise to be is yet another step. I've never run a marathon, but even with my bad attitude I have run a number of half marathons over the years and I'm convinced that it is the measure of the marathon itself that is a key driver of its pursuit. If you go running for an hour, you naturally check how far you have run, particularly given how easy the GPS system on your phone and readily available tracking apps make it to do so. As you get into the habit of running you notice that you are running further in the same time or running for longer more easily. You notice that you've already covered a quarter, a third or a half of a marathon and you just start to think: 'Yes, I could do that!', even if you might be much better off taking a break at that stage and hitting the weights room next time instead.

Marilyn Strathern memorably suggested that 'When a measure becomes a target it ceases to be a good measure.'[1] The metrics that we use can become dangerous when we treat them as targets to pursue rather than indicators from which to learn. It is always possible to reach a target by distorted means. Circumstances may change, rendering a particular target counter-productive. And ill-chosen targets may cause us to take for granted the appropriateness of actions we might otherwise never have even considered worthwhile or useful.

When we choose inappropriate targets or stick rigidly to measures that may previously have been useful but are no longer right for changing conditions, this can create distortions that not only imperil the enterprise but ultimately may cost us all. The measures of success in business have for too long been too narrow in scope, to the detriment of both enterprise and the society it serves.

Changing measures of business success

Happiness is best found not by trying to be happy, but as an outcome of striving to live a meaningful life. Similarly, while a business needs money to fuel its activities, if its only purpose is to make a profit it will likely fall short of its potential and fail to sustain its profits for the long-term anyway.

Increases in shareholder value are an excellent *outcome* for an enterprise. When assessed in context they are also a good *indicator* of performance. They are however a poor *target*. As we saw previously, *maximising* shareholder value as an *exclusive* goal is an awful target. And enshrining shareholder value maximisation as the exclusive target for *all* businesses may be viewed by some as one of the greatest errors in the history of economics.

André Gide memorably wrote in his *Les Nourritures Terrestres*, or *Fruits of the Earth,* that 'every creature indicates the presence of God, but none reveals him. As soon as we stop to look at that one creature alone, it distracts us from God.'[2] We can appropriate the thought and apply it to purpose and metrics (sorry, André!); although all indicators can offer valuable information from which to draw insight, as soon as we get stuck on any particular indicator at the expense of our holistic vision, it diminishes our capacity to succeed. This then leads to distorted outcomes that can, over time, cause tremendous harm. This is often not even recognised until it is too late for the damage to be recovered.

The often-cited observation that you get what you measure can be taken as a cautionary tale. The history of business failures is replete with enterprises whose leaders succumbed to chasing spurious targets. Using such targets to drive repeated cycles of maladaptive change caused the rapid demise of those businesses. We can think of businesses in the dot-com boom chasing clicks and eyeballs but failing to have a plan to convert interest into sustainable value-exchange. Or businesses focused on quarterly reporting to the detriment of long-term value creation, manipulating the timing and degree of investment not on the basis of what will be most useful for driving innovation for sustainable growth but on the basis of what will show the best returns in the very short run. Research appears to show, for example, that increasing the number of financial analysts tracking a particular industry actually reduces investment in new patents across that industry by diverting management to achieving quarterly earnings targets rather than building the long-term future of the enterprise.[3] The greatest consequence of ill-chosen targets and the absence in a business's accounts of an assessment of the overall impact of its activities is of course that the societal contribution of a business remains un-optimised, to the potentially great detriment of all.

A new narrative-based meta-purpose for enterprise is therefore needed to provide a conceptual framework within which organisations can achieve, measure and communicate greater purposeful growth as well as enhance their capacity to adapt as the conditions in which they operate change and reveal new problems to solve.

Unlocking shared ambition

The wealth created by a business is not limited to increases in shareholder value. It can also be understood in terms of the total societal change it serves to bring about. A business can thrive because we need and love the difference it can make to our lives.

Businesses create positive societal value that reaches beyond their customers to colleagues, partners, communities and the broader environment in which they operate. This value can be intentionally increased and can lead to greater trust, commitment and support for the enterprise.

Today, most businesses do not have a way of assessing the total value that they create or even whether they are a net force for good or for harm in the world. In fact, early research conducted by George Serafeim at Harvard Business School may show that a frightening proportion of businesses do indeed do more harm than good.

Failing to ground a business strategy in the intention to

create social value causes its leaders not only to miss crucial opportunities to better serve their stakeholders but also to overlook their greatest potential for success in so doing. Our customers benefit by receiving a greater service; our communities benefit from more inclusive outcomes; and staff benefit from the satisfaction that comes from doing something worthwhile. Businesses benefit in turn from being more useful to more people because their own success inevitably depends upon the decisions and actions of people outside the business, as well as on the discretionary effort, motivation and engagement of the people they employ. This aligns stakeholders through enterprise for shared rewards and purposeful outcomes.

Creating a Wealth of Change

Organisations are not ends in their own right. They are tools that we create to better meet our needs. They cannot function outside a supportive environment with the infrastructure on which they depend. And their impacts can reach beyond owners, staff and even customers to affect us all.

I therefore propose the Wealth of Change to refer to the value of the total change created through an enterprise by its stakeholders.

Just as the chance to enjoy a conversation with a friend is more valuable than the coffee that may go with it, a night out with the girls may be more fun than the bar that happens to accommodate it, and designing the architecture of the future may be more inspiring than the computer-aided design (CAD) software used to create it, the greatest change will be the change we can empower our customers and other groups to make for themselves. The success of our customers is therefore a pre-requisite for our own viability. Indeed, businesses cannot achieve anything directly, but can be used as tools to create change by their investors, leaders, employees, partners, customers and communities. We can empower each of these groups to join us in creating our Wealth of Change.

This builds, among other observations, on advances in understanding developed by Nobel prize-winning development economist Amartya Sen. Sen argues for a capabilities-based approach to development that focuses on expanding people's capacity to become or to act, rather than on leaving them unsupported in the name of non-interference or simply shielding them from the exterior effects of their problems. He sees development as a tool that should be used to expand freedom, with a focus on what people can be supported in being 'free to' do, not just what they can be protected in order to be 'free from'.[4] Thinking about value as a form of empowerment that expands the range of things we can do can be as useful for an individual enterprise as it can for a nation's approach to economic development. When we empower our stakeholders, we can say that thanks to our work, people are able to better fulfil their aspirations in life.

Empowering particular stakeholder groups alone, however, is not enough. In a recent case, the carbon-negative BrewDog lost valuable support for its highly aspirational mission when it emerged that its widely celebrated climate-friendly priorities were undermined by a perception among staff of an internal culture of aggression and intolerance.[5] As well as ensuring that we empower desired positive change for one stakeholder group, we must also seek to avoid creating harm for other stakeholders, that could cause our net Wealth of Change to be diminished or negative and make it harder to justify the existence of our enterprise, let alone the support of many of the people on which it may depend.

Businesses benefit from fostering a purpose that is shared across stakeholder groups because their success inevitably depends upon the decisions and actions of a wide range of people outside the business as well as on the discretionary effort, motivation and engagement of the people whom they employ. Many leaders and entrepreneurs know this instinctively. When Andrew Hunt launched his baobab range of fruit bars for example, he didn't just focus on commercial success (good for his enterprise), or even on the delicious taste and health benefits of the bars (good for retailers and consumers), but he also realised that if he could make a market for the African super-fruit in the west it could bring billions of dollars of income to rural African farmers. This insight ultimately landed him the might of the United Nations as a supporter in growing his business (great for his enterprise).

The Wealth of Change versus change management

Historically the analysis of change in business has largely focused on 'change management'. Driven by an inward-looking view of the business alone, under the influence of the primacy of shareholder value and the concept of competitive advantage, change management has focused on change that can be controlled within a business rather than enabled by the business in the outside world. Analysis by the economist John Greenhough found that 95 per cent of worldwide MBA content today focuses its analysis inside the business rather than on the world in which it operates. We may be training business leaders in myopia on a global scale. Indeed, according to the World Benchmarking Alliance, the majority of businesses, even among those who have signed up for their impact benchmarking, do not even have due diligence mechanisms in place to understand many of the broader social impacts of their operations.[6] The result is that much of the full potential role of businesses' products and services in their customers' lives as well as the total societal impact of their activities remain in most cases hidden from view and underutilised as tools for innovation, engagement and growth.

An outward-facing approach to understanding the change created by business in the world outside, however, opens the door to business that is both more exciting and creates greater value for all whom it serves.

Creating a Wealth of Change lends itself to the incorporation of insights and techniques that may not commonly be associated with business, including approaches from the non-profit world, such as the Theory of Change. The Theory of Change is a methodology used to promote social change by starting from the identification of a desired end point and working backwards from there to explore what is needed to achieve that end point, without a priori assumptions about the role of the organisation in achieving the change.

Theory of Change-inspired questions might include:

- What is the changing nature of the world in which our customers and other stakeholders live and work?
- What changes do the people we serve and those most important to them now most need or aspire to achieve?
- What is currently missing that stops this from being possible or fully achievable?
- Where are there still obstacles to making this available?
- What role can we play in overcoming these obstacles and filling these emergent gaps?
- How can we make these changes more self-perpetuating for stakeholders? And more sustainable for the enterprise?

- How should this change our organisational priorities?
- How should we adapt existing capabilities and propositions, or where necessary develop new capabilities and propositions to meet these priorities?
- What approach to metrics and accountability will help us measure, evaluate and improve our success as we go?

Defining the Wealth of Change

The key challenge in defining the Wealth of Change for an individual enterprise is to identify an inclusive purpose that demonstrates how the enterprise seeks to achieve a positive change in the world. Such a purpose aligns the interests of stakeholders so that their needs become sympathetic to each other rather than potentially antagonistic. Trade-off is replaced by reciprocity, mutuality and the generation of new value creation. This integration of purpose can be harnessed to drive business performance and stakeholder engagement.

Previously Unilever's 'Simple' brand framed its purpose as being 'Kind to skin'. This served to create a customer benefit but risked doing so at a cost to broader society through the environmental impact of the brand's products and packaging. Repurposing Simple to be 'Kind to people, planet and skin' was both intuitive to customers and opened the door to an array of win–win outcomes. The positive message facilitated a brand partnership with Little Mix to combat the bullying of teenagers online and foster kinder relationships through their #choosekindness campaign. It opened the door to new product development opportunities including biodegradable face wipes that users can even compost themselves in forty-two days. And it gave the brand's management teams an exciting role to play in advancing Unilever's broader purpose of making good living commonplace. At the time of writing this passage, three-quarters of Unilever's growth comes from brands with a social dimension to their purpose and these brands are growing 70 per cent faster than Unilever's other brands.

The Five Stakeholder Dividends Framework

The Wealth of Change identifies the total societal value that an enterprise empowers. It can retain a portion of that value in profits and shareholder returns, enabling re-investment and attracting new investment in a positive cycle. But as all stakeholders are active co-determinants of the Wealth of Change that is achieved, it makes sense to identify the rewards that each stakeholder can retain from the value that they collectively create. A 'dividend' literally means something to be divided. In supporting enterprises in purpose-led growth, I therefore adapt the notion of a 'shareholder dividend' and extend it across all stakeholder groups through the Five Stakeholder Dividends Framework to identify rewards for all of a business's stakeholder groups.

These include:

- Customer Dividend: The improvements enabled in customers' lives
- Employee Dividend: Not just remuneration but also growth and fulfilment.
- Partner Dividend: The outcomes that partners are empowered to achieve
- Community Dividend: The benefits that cascade across communities
- Planetary Dividend: The regeneration of our shared environment

In analysing each Stakeholder Dividend, we can identify how the creation of the Stakeholder Dividend in turn also drives the purposeful growth of the business and thereby creates a Shareholder Dividend, not just literally in the form of a distributed profit per share, but also metaphorically in terms of growth in value and alignment with broader investor objectives. Just as we benefit each stakeholder group, we also gain from their active participation in a reciprocal exchange.

Examples in practice might include:

How the TrainMore chain of gyms shows that it is on the side of its customers in their hope of improving their fitness levels. TrainMore creates a **Customer Dividend** by offering its members a one-euro reduction to their monthly subscription for each day that they train, helping customers make better use of their gyms and leading to greater loyalty, faster recruitment, more active referrals and better uptake of additional products and services from a more committed membership. Creating greater customer benefits ties, perhaps unsurprisingly, to greater enterprise success. Enterprises in the top 20 per cent of the American Customer Satisfaction Index, for example, earned just under double the Dow Jones Industrial Average over the period from 1997 to 2003.[7]

How Recycling Lives creates an **Employee Dividend** by replicating their warehouse in local prisons where they give prisoners the option of earning money while being trained to dismantle electronic and other goods for recycling and have the option of employment with the business when they are released. Ninety-five per cent of prisoners in the UK leave prison at some point; 60 per cent of these re-offend, but this drops to 5 per cent in the case of prisoners employed by Recycling Lives. This means that Recycling Lives indeed lives up to its name in turning lives around and protecting

THE WEALTH OF CHANGE

society from the costs of recidivism. The social value that Recycling Lives creates helps them to win commercial contracts, meaning that turning lives around also drives the success of the business. While this may be a particularly compelling example, the evidence suggests that Employee Dividends work across any sector. Professor Alex Edmans found that the 100 Best Companies to Work For in America[8] delivered stock returns that beat their peers by an average of 2.3 to 3.8 per cent per year over a twenty-eight year period, unlocking an 89 per cent to 184 per cent cumulative differential growth rate.[9]

How Santander creates a **Partner Dividend** through its work with Alzheimer's Society in its quest to become the UK's most dementia-friendly bank. After a diagnosis of dementia, some of the biggest concerns people affected by the illness most commonly express relate to finances. The illness can be costly to live with, and increasing numbers of criminal operations intentionally target people affected with dementia with fraud. More than a million people in the UK currently live with dementia, and often struggle to access and manage their finances, creating further vulnerability. Santander has therefore partnered with Alzheimer's Society to audit its operations, including customer journeys in branch and through contact centres and how it supports employees who may have caring responsibilities. Santander has committed to raising 1.5 million pounds for Alzheimer's Society through a Memory Walk and Dementia Friends Programme, and at the time of writing is already well on track to hit that target. It also extends the reach of the small charity to benefit the lives of Santander's staff and customer base. But it also turns out that what people affected by dementia mostly need is simpler banking processes, which can create benefits for all customers. Who among us would choose a bank for its complicated practices? As Elisa Moscolin, head of sustainability at Santander UK tells me, 'If we get it right for vulnerable customers, we get it right

157

for everyone. We want to be a simple, personal and fair bank and that ambition is true for all our customers: the recommendations from Alzheimer's Society to simplify our processes can improve all our customer experiences.' Our ability to work in partnership across the business ecosystems in which we operate is increasingly becoming the determining factor of our success.

How Airbnb creates a **Community Dividend** by working with its member hosts to enable any one of us to 'belong anywhere in the world'. It does so by rivalling the largest hotel chains with a radical alternative model which allows property owners to rent out their spare rooms to paying guests. As Douglas Atkin, former Head of Community at Airbnb, has put it to me, the need to belong is so hardwired into our survival instincts that we suffer the pain of social exclusion in the same way that we suffer the pain of a wound or injury. He was recruited in part thanks to the organising role he had played in the first presidential election campaign for Barack Obama. The quest to achieve Airbnb's shared purpose with its members was perceived by its leadership more like a political campaign or non-profit than a conventional brand-managed community, drawing as it did on community managers who worked like activists in empowering members to drive change. This approach has enabled Airbnb to achieve global growth unconstrained by a need to invest in property. More broadly, businesses can invest in community involvement to meet specific needs in their local area, contribute to economic development, build capacity in a particular sector, or make a location more desirable and vibrant. The returns on community investment can address material concerns such as building a talent pool, raising corporate and brand awareness, creating future markets or aligning with particular local or customer interests. Non-profits can also create reciprocal relationships through better community development. A social enterprise that I have worked with in addressing loneliness among seniors, for example, switched its growth strategy from geographic expansion to geographic intensification, engaging with communities as a whole to create 'loneliness-free neighbourhoods'.

How Loop creates a **Planetary Dividend** by offering zero-waste versions of everyday products from people's favourite brands that can be delivered to the doorstep in reusable packaging in place of a conventional supermarket order. This gives them access to a committed customer base of eco-friendly shoppers keen to improve their environmental impact while still enjoying the groceries they love. Research shows that a planetary dividend is effective in unlocking superior financial returns. An indicator of 'eco efficiency' from Innovest Strategic Advisors measures the value of a company's goods and services in relation to the waste that it causes. Highly rated stocks beat low-ranked ones by 5 per cent per year between 1995 and 2003.[10]

It is also important to recognise that investors can also not just put their money into an enterprise but through their monitoring and engagement processes can actively support the success of the business. A healthy relationship between an enterprise and its investors multiplies the benefits to all parties by better harnessing the generative potential of their collective capabilities.

The Wealth of Change can be adapted to address the priorities and stakeholder environments of government bodies and non-profit organisations to model how they can achieve sustainable change through mutually valuable relationships. The important aspect is to identify an inclusive shared purpose and the sustainable reciprocal exchanges among stakeholders that can drive it while unlocking self-directed rewards as needed.

Measuring the Wealth of Change

The more holistic view involved in creating a Wealth of Change widens the approach we need to take to metrics with a greater emphasis on stakeholder (rather than only shareholder) accountability. It lends itself to narrative indicators and also to feed-forward rather than just feedback mechanisms so that an enterprise can better revitalise and repurpose its activities to address the emergent realities of its stakeholders.

Conventional approaches to accounting draw up an analysis of internal change for management, fiduciary, government and investor reporting obligations. As we have identified, however, the far bigger story is the story of change taking place outside the enterprise, including the direct changes that the enterprise enables its customers and other stakeholders to make. Forms of accountability that contextualise and explain outcomes and their implications for future activity and growth can therefore serve a purpose in uniting a wide range of contributors who can be drawn into this more ambitious process of positive change.

We are already beginning to see a broadening of approaches to accountability, as leading global corporations have first begun to publish CSR reports to cover a wider range of social and environmental impacts and then to integrate these reports into their main annual reports as made available to investors and to the public. We also see progress towards understanding the net societal contribution of businesses that factor in environmental and even social costs through techniques such as true cost or full cost accounting, the application of GRI (Global Reporting Initiative) standards[11] or Science-Based Targets[12] to improve climate action.

And in the non-profit world we are seeing a move away from linear reporting primarily for the benefit of donors and grant funders to more dynamic reporting that involves all actors in understanding and contributing to change in real time.[13]

Whereas conventional accountability has been a linear process, focused on analysis of internal performance for a limited audience, accountability is increasingly becoming a process of involving all stakeholders in collectively understanding, formulating and achieving shared purpose through dynamic interaction and real-time adjustment. It helps us not only measure the success that we have achieved but also identify the basis for future improvements in that success and even to further redefine what success must look like.

However, there is still a long way to go. How many businesses set targets that their customers and other communities would like to see them achieve or even actively support them in achieving? And how much value is left uncreated as a result? Many business leaders reduce the story of their business to its value in annual revenue or profit – 'I run a 20-million-pound business' or a '100-million-pound business'. But who apart from the owners of the business cares about that? The Eden Project in Cornwall tracks the total value of the tourism that it brings to the region. This currently stands at over £2.2 billion. Now *that* is a powerful measure to engage the support of communities, partners and government! By working with the concept of the Wealth of Change and identifying stakeholder dividends that feed into it we can identify and achieve worthwhile outcomes that involve and empower all the groups with whom our success must be achieved and therefore should be shared.

Efficiency versus effectiveness

Much value has been lost in recent decades in chasing efficiency at the expense of effectiveness. If we suppose that the purpose of an enterprise is to direct the resources it owns, manages or controls to achieve a superior financial return, then the overwhelming focus of internal effort becomes the pursuit of efficiency savings.

Each day, month or year that passes, we track, monitor, analyse and evaluate our methods of production and value creation to streamline them, to increase their rate of production and to reduce their associated costs. While this can initially make a useful contribution to the bottom line, when performed repeatedly over time without being shaped by a larger context of changing needs, this approach creates hidden vulnerabilities: the very efficiency of production actively prevents the preservation and accumulation of the human capacity to adapt and repurpose.

For many businesses, the efficiency of low cash reserves, stocks and just-in-time supply chains left them exposed by the pandemic in ways that diminished their resilience. As Ian Goldin has said to me, 'One of the reasons that banks were so vulnerable during the financial crisis and one of the reasons we see a crisis today in supply chains is due to just-in-time processes driven by quarterly reports to analysts who believe that working capital not used is working capital wasted. This maximises throughput and minimises spare capacity which is a recipe for fragility.'

Efficiency at the expense of effectiveness can also cause trouble in publicly funded institutions. In the early weeks of the pandemic in the UK, for example, we discovered that the very efficiency of the National Health Service in terms of its high rate of bed use, a figure that had previously been cited with pride as superior to the rate found in other nations, and an example of effective resource allocation with minimum wastage, became a significant vulnerability in the face of a sharp rise in demand from an unexpected source of need. Indeed, the discharge of thousands of elderly patients into care homes ill-equipped to receive them safely in order to maintain bed-use efficiency – and without testing them for COVID – was ultimately found to be unlawful in the High Court and was described by Jason Coppel QC, the barrister representing the plaintifs as 'one of the most egregious and devastating policy failures in the modern era'.[14]

Such distortions of efficiency become increasingly significant as they scale. When everyone pursues the same target the unwanted effects of the distortion can reach their most serious consequences. To ensure that efficiency is not achieved at the expense of effectiveness requires an outward-looking focus that factors in a broad range of purposeful qualitative indicators and is ever-vigilant to the need for renewal.

The measure of money

Money is perhaps the most powerful and influential measure ever invented. But more than it is a measure, even money is a story. Over 90 per cent of the world's money exists only as numbers on servers. Even physical banknotes have no intrinsic value. In the words of each British bank note, they are a 'promise to pay the bearer on demand'. The numbers that represent our money are just notions of value based on narratives of trust, ideas and relationships. If those ideas, trust and relationships fall apart, the story changes and the value that the money represents collapses with them. Vladimir Putin, for example, discovered that following his invastion of Ukraine he was unable to use the $630 billion foreign currency reserves he had built up because they were frozen in the banks where they were held.[15]

Economies did not develop to create profit, but to enable the exchange of capabilities. Money is not an intrinsic good. Rather it was invented as a tool to solve a set of problems. It offers a form of cooperation born of the need to reconcile competing interests through reciprocal exchange, at scale and among all-comers, not just members of our own tribe or locals. When someone you know and trust asks you for one of your cows, you can give it to them if you can spare it, knowing that in a future of unpredictable problems you will be able to call on a valuable favour in return. The problem arises, however, when you want to ask a favour of someone who may never see you again. A mechanism of on-the-spot exchange becomes necessary that effectively enables the fulfilment of the request to be converted into something that can be exchanged at any future point for any good from any person.

Money has become a great enabler of human development, empowering our ever more complex global economy and allowing us to participate in systems of worldwide cooperation. If money didn't exist, we'd have to re-invent it immediately to continue with almost any aspect of our lives as we know them. Indeed, the concept of money is already being re-invented in a number of ways, whether through money-creation by bank lending without matching deposits, sovereign monetary policy or digital currencies, all of which change the story of what money is in the first place.*

---

* Plans currently exist to create a new 'Britcoin' that would be a Bank of England-backed electronic currency for the UK, enabling digital transactions without the risks associated with independent cryptocurrencies.

An intriguing historic example reveals that the story of financial value is itself largely part of a much bigger story of status. Between 1813 and 1815, the Prussian royal family urged all citizens to contribute their jewellery to fund the uprising against Napoleon during the War of Liberation. People who donated their gold and silver jewellery were given replicas of the items that they offered made of iron. As a consequence, wearing gold and silver jewellery became a symbol of selfishness and involved a loss of status, while wearing iron jewellery became a mark of patriotic virtue. The story determined the status that wearing jewellery was intended to achieve and thereby transferred the value of achieving that status from one form of jewellery to another. Sacrificing wealth rather than displaying it became key to achieving a higher standing in society and more favourable relationships with one's peers.

If strategy is left to a financial view to orchestrate it without that view itself fitting into a greater narrative, the risk is that it can become too inward-looking. Money simplifies our understanding of value creation in ways that can be distorting. As with all currencies, the notion of the 'Great British Pound' requires all pounds to have equal exchange value: but of course, all pounds are not *created* equally. If an unusually frank teenager asks for advice on which is better, earning a hundred pounds a day on an apprenticeship or stealing bicycles and selling them on, although the latter certainly offers a low-cost high-margin transaction, you know full well what advice you ought to give. But when it comes to the economy, we simplify our understanding to chase financial growth in ways that are largely blind to the implications of how the wealth is generated and constituted, the impacts of those processes on society and the future value-creation opportunities those processes are enabling or inhibiting.*

My father told me as a child the story of a customer at the branch of a bank he had worked in earlier in his life. The customer seemed a charming gentleman. He came into the bank and gave the clerks handy betting tips as he paid in the cash from his bookmakers' business and withdrew cheques for his overheads. Little did they know that he also had an account at a different bank in which he paid in the cheques from his fine art dealership and withdrew cash for his expenses. Or that he had an account at a further bank for the fish and chip shop he ran with his wife. Most of all, they did not know that all these businesses were fictional. He was simply moving money between the accounts at each of his three banks.

In those days, credit-worthiness was determined largely not by the amount of money a depositor had in their account but rather by the flow of funds they moved through the account. All three of this customer's 'businesses' were therefore deemed credit-worthy and he began to take out loans. Cycling ever larger sums through the accounts, he made effective payment installments on these loans, further elevating his credit-worthiness until he was able to take out the maximum allowable loan from all three banks: at which point he quietly disappeared.

* Interestingly, as we saw in Chapter One, not only are all pounds not created equally, but the benefit to us in human happiness of receiving them is not equal either. Further studies include a Gallup poll of 1.7 million people from around the world in 2010, which confirms that the return on happiness for additional increases of income decreases once our key needs are met. This reflects most human sensory functions, few of which are linear. See 'Happiness, income satiation and turning points around the world', by Andrew T. Jebb, Louis Tay, Ed Diener and Shigehiro Oishi, in *Nature Human Behaviour*, 2018 Jan 2(1) 33–38.

He has since never been heard of by the banks. He did not even become a wanted criminal, as the banks chose not to notify the authorities as they had not yet found better ways to protect themselves from potential copycat fraudsters. But the story of his antics does show how making money and creating value are not the same thing.

It is easy to see a parallel to our bank fraudster in a consumer economy that has grown on the back of extracting from nature more value than is created as a result, and implicating us in the fraud by, as Tim Jackson puts it to me, 'gaslighting' us into thinking that we need it to be happy. We can also see a parallel with the process of financialisation, through which financial services firms are simply creating value for each other without changing anything in the 'real' economy. This creates hidden vulnerabilities in the economy when the perceptions on which this 'value' rests become shaken, as in the 2008 financial collapse, when the perception of the value of home loans was downgraded, setting in motion a domino effect that has severely impacted lives all around the globe ever since.[16]

Changing measures of economic success

Distortions caused by measurement are too often also present in the way we understand the economy as a whole and in the approaches that we take to growing it. The observation that all pounds are not created equally and do not therefore offer the same value to present and future realities is largely hidden from view in the way we organise our national accounts. Even when we ask seemingly simple questions, such as 'is our economy expanding or shrinking?', we find that important context needed to give a true picture is missing and the apparent objectivity of the numbers can be powerfully misleading. To what degree, for example, did measures of our national accounts in 2019 factor in the hidden risk of our vulnerability to the pandemic? What vision of national life do our measures of economic value and growth seek to orientate us towards in the first place?

The key indicators at the heart of national accounts were devised by the economist John Maynard Keynes during World War II to support industrial mobilisation in support of the war effort.[17] We needed to know how much materiel and other supplies we could produce to determine and resource our military strategy. The system was never intended to be a permanent or complete approach to understanding the economy and its development. Our reliance on it to this day causes us to misunderstand the true nature of the economy; to distort our approaches to economic development; and to lack a broader vision of purpose for economic development to serve.

With the existence of measures such as gross domestic product (GDP) we can easily assume that if the figure rises, this is a good thing and if the figure stagnates or falls it is a bad thing – and with all things being equal that may be true. The trouble is that *ceteris paribus*, the economist's universal opt-out clause, is, as we saw previously, always a false assumption. All things are never equal and, separated from the context that generates them, the numbers can tell a clear but distorting story.

Criticisms of the national accounting system are often based on the observation that the link between economic growth and human wellbeing may not be stable and direct. While some forms of economic growth may be harmful to human wellbeing and others may contribute to it disproportionately, GDP has no inherent mechanism for us to discriminate between these occurrences. GDP also fails to account for services on which society depends but which by their nature often take place in contexts that are unpaid, such as child-rearing, cooking and cleaning. They also exclude much of the output of government and charities: yet these activities are directly intended to provide social and collective benefits, and are likely to contribute more on average to our shared wellbeing than a similar resource mobilisation for purely private ends. The result is that much economic activity is under-valued and under-supported, while arguably some value-creation is undoubtedly over-rewarded from the perspective of the economy as a whole and the society it is intended to serve.

More comprehensive metrics have been developed to measure national wellbeing across a broader range of dimensions, including environmental, physical, mental, work, social and political factors as well as economic ones. New Zealand launched a 'wellbeing budget' in 2019; Bhutan enshrined the pursuit of Gross National Happiness in the constitution of its government in 2008; and nations including the United Kingdom are exploring broader measures for tracking economic progress. The United Nations Development Programme has maintained its Human Development Index over the past three decades to influence policy-making with a wider lens on economic development and has in recent years integrated environmental issues. I also particularly like the work that Michael Green has pioneered on the creation of a Social Progress Index that measures society's ability to meet the needs of its members through the assessment of over fifty social and environmental indicators that track actual life outcomes of national populations over time, enabling new priorities to be identified and addressed.[18] Norway topped the rankings in 2021, with the United Kingdom coming in eighteenth place and the United States in twenty-fourth out of 168 countries assessed.

In Part Three we'll take a deeper dive into a number of enterprises that have achieved a Purpose Upgrade and develop a comprehensive approach to implementing a Purpose Upgrade in your own business.

For your enterprise

- **How is purpose defined, measured, evaluated and enhanced in your organisation?**
- **How free, empowered and motivated are people inside and outside your organisation to contribute to your purpose?**
- **What opportunities do you create to re-enliven or redefine your purpose? How does this work at all levels within the organisation? When new problems arise, (how) is purpose renewed?**

Part Three

THE PRACTICE

Chapter Six

PURPOSE REDISCOVERED

Leaders around the world are already unlocking the rewards of Purpose Upgrades across organisations of every size, sector and territory, ranging from small community-minded social enterprises to global publicly traded corporations. Indeed, a Purpose Upgrade has underpinned many of the most effective business turnarounds and breakthrough successes of recent years. And this trend is likely to accelerate in the years to come as incumbent business and operating models become more urgently unviable.

To fulfill the potential of a Purpose Upgrade requires both the commitment of leaders and the participation of the stakeholders of a business at all levels. It involves re-defining the core nature of the problems that the business addresses. It provides new pathways for stakeholders inside and outside the enterprise to pursue in solving those problems. And it reaches a new set of outcomes that include all relevant stakeholders in sharing the rewards of success.

The first-hand perspectives of pioneering leaders illuminate the challenges that this can involve and the outcomes that can be achieved.

Applying a Purpose Upgrade across an enterprise

While a Purpose Upgrade can be applied to any activity within an enterprise, or more broadly to any activity within our sphere of control or influence, it can often unlock its most powerful results for business by repurposing an enterprise as a whole. As Feike Sijbesma, Honorary Chair and former CEO of Royal DSM, tells me:

> Companies should think about how they can be meaningful in the core of their business, in their core competencies, in their core business model and in their core revenues. If you don't do anything good for the world with your core offerings you should ask yourself if you are futureproof. If the world doesn't really need you, your investors are increasingly likely to find this out even before you do.

Many of the greatest turnarounds of performance in corporate history have involved a Purpose Upgrade. For example, Satya Nadella's greatly admired tenure as CEO of Microsoft began with his candid recognition that the tech giant had lost its way. The company's leaders had lost sight of why Microsoft should exist. It had left new opportunities in smartphones, tablet and web services to the likes of Google and Amazon to pursue, missing out on the mobile revolution and getting stuck in a cycle of pushing the Windows Operating System onto customers who had increasingly moved on, in order to hit internal sales targets rather than seek out and discover true stakeholder needs.

Nadella had originally joined the company with a desire to be part of a group of people who felt that they were on a mission to change the world, reasoning that he would spend far too much time working to be content for that work to lack meaning. When he took over as CEO, Nadella's solution was therefore to implement a Purpose Upgrade, through which he re-defined Microsoft's purpose in a mission to 'empower every person and every organisation on the planet to achieve more'.[1] He saw in this quest the means to unleash fresh energy, new ideas and a deep renewal, overcoming the blind spots, sunk costs and plan continuation biases that had built up over the years and taking a very different approach to future growth.

He used the new purpose to unite opposing factions within the business in embracing rather than resisting change; to redirect innovation into emerging cloud-based services; and to extend the reach of Microsoft's software across the competitor and open-source platforms to which its customers had migrated. At the time of writing, Microsoft's market capitalisation has just passed $2 trillion for the first time, having risen 700 per cent since Nadella took over. This means that 90 per cent of the current value of the company has been created under his leadership and through the pursuit of the new purpose that he identified.

This approach certainly made it easier to identify the right roles for Microsoft to play during the pandemic, such as enabling telemedicine, crisis information-sharing, better management of critical supplies and better tracking of Covid cases in real-time, as well as using AI to triage people concerned about potential symptoms and freeing up doctors and other healthcare workers to provide critical care where it was most needed. Addressing economic as well as health challenges, Microsoft supported the shift to remote working, and empowered schools and universities to move their courses online, often in a matter of days, as well as helping people to defend against cyber-attacks and fraud intended to take advantage of the angst caused by the virus. The business also provided emergency funds to local communities and made many of its offerings free to non-profits for extended periods.

Nadella's turnaround at Microsoft is not an isolated example. An article in *Harvard Business Review* identified purpose-level change as the driving factor in the top twenty business turnarounds of the last decade, citing access to new growth, a repositioning of the core and strong financial performance as key indicators of success[2] and arguing that 'the decision to infuse a higher purpose into the culture[. . .] has propelled these companies to success'. Examples included Netflix repurposing from delivering existing content to creating Oscar-worthy original content, multiplying its profits thirty-two-fold in the process; China's AIA Group shifting from providing insurance to enabling wellness through a preventative health mission and achieving compound annual growth of 15 per cent since 2013; and Tencent Holdings, shifting from catering to users' basic online needs to 'improving the quality of human life through digital innovation', fulfilling the aspiration by investing in education, entertainment, autonomous vehicles and fintech, all of which contributed to Tencent becoming the first Asian company to surpass a 500-billion-dollar market valuation.

A deeper dive into three cases can illustrate the potential of a Purpose Upgrade in diverse sectors and at radically different sizes of enterprise, as well as some of the challenges that this can involve.

From volunteering to systems change

Repurposing often involves looking outside the confines of our current scope of work. That kind of peripheral vision can often also be fostered by stepping outside the day job.

As a younger marketer I often enjoyed offering my skills to particular charities or social enterprises close to my heart. I also realised that at a time of increasing interest in social and environmental issues, other marketers might enjoy doing the same. I therefore created a matching platform that works rather like the online dating of pro bono marketing to make that kind of experience more readily available to other marketers. The aim of the platform is to market a better world. And it has now supported over 3,000 charities and social enterprises with access to pro bono marketing to do just that.

Running the platform provided a revealing counterpart to my own advisory work at the Agency of the Future. I came to think of it as a living laboratory of Collaborative Advantage in practice and many of the insights I learned through the platform and the relationships and progress it unlocked informed the development of my first book, which proposed the concept. Our causes are typically run by 'Ninjas' of higher purpose, each relentlessly dedicated to the particular cause that brought their organisation into being. Even small charities and social enterprises typically have relatively complex stakeholder environments when you factor in their beneficiaries, service users, volunteers, ambassadors, donors, grant-providers and partners. And then in came our marketers with their tools of creativity and influence, and applied those tools to the cause purpose to unlock greater collective change across those stakeholder groups by aligning their interests around common goals. It taught me much of what I needed to know about making the shift from the goal of creating Competitive Advantage to Collaborative Advantage.

It also taught me about the value of human agency and the importance of empowering changes that people create for themselves. While I originally thought that our non-profit improved marketers' capabilities, that support from marketers improved our causes, and that our causes improved people's lives, I came ultimately to the conclusion that this was an incomplete picture. Our charities and social enterprises typically do something better than improving people's lives: they create contexts in which people can improve their own lives, which is key to how they create sustainable and self-perpetuating change. A community kitchen that provides meals and good company once a week to vulnerable and often older beneficiaries at risk of the effects of exclusion won't solve their problems for them. But it can give people a way to be noticed, with the knowledge that friendly faces are expecting them and that there is something to look forward to, a new routine to build on and a starting point for making new friends. Plus it serves as a reminder of the value of eating healthy food at a time when they may otherwise simply have lost the will to bother amid the loneliness and isolation that they have experienced. In contrast to a conventional economic approach that might seek to identify the most financially efficient way to supply an optimal range of macro-nutrients to someone in food poverty, this community kitchen addresses a whole-person problem with a socialised solution that empowers self-directed change.

Similarly, our marketers don't directly change cause outcomes. More accurately, they work with our causes to create the narratives they can use themselves to drive change for months, and in many cases years, to come. And while we do not actively train our marketers in the conventional way, giving them bigger and more meaningful problems to solve brings with it the chance to reconsider and re-appraise what they are capable of as marketers and the difference they can make to the world. It enables them to pursue marketing as a vocation and to change their own story of who they are as professionals and change-makers. The platform became an impact multiplier, enabling thousands of marketers to drive change, which in turn enabled thousands of causes to unlock far greater change through their own activities; and which in turn has enabled millions of their collective beneficiaries to bring about change in their own lives and the lives of their loved ones.

As with any organisation, as times moved on, elements of our purpose needed to change too, to better reflect new levels of aspiration made possible by our changing environment, track record and deepening relationships.

In particular, when COVID-19 struck, the need for many of our causes to provide front-line support went sky high, but their opportunities for funding fell through the floor. In many instances they do the majority of their fundraising at a single annual event. In 2020, not only were the events and their associated donations cancelled, but many charities also had already committed to the costs of running their events, meaning their annual income was replaced by a significant uncovered expenditure.

At the same time, marketers in business were confronting a complex array of social and environmental issues, with prominent movements for change emerging, ranging from the Me Too and Black Lives Matter campaigns to Extinction Rebellion. And this really was only the tip of the iceberg. Businesses that are not in some way contributing to increased equity and inclusion and actively reducing the impact of the climate emergency and environmental resource depletion are making the world worse, not better. The whole basis of marketers' day jobs was in question. Capitalism needed to be recreated. New meta-narratives were needed to guide business and society alike.

We therefore came to believe that marketing as a profession has a much stronger role to play in better advancing humankind and not just through individual actions. Most global challenges are also marketing problems in disguise. You can't solve issues like rising inequality, resource depletion and climate change, without unprecedented levels of human understanding, cooperation and the creative ideas that hold these together.

Repurposing didn't mean losing our original platform. We continue to this day to run the matching service connecting marketing volunteers with causes in an online dating of pro bono marketing. But it did mean expanding the mission to progress from individual professionals marketing a better world to a collective of marketers working together to build creative solutions to human problems: our own Purpose Upgrade in response to greater need and the opportunity to meet it.

We changed the name of the social enterprise to MarketingKind and the new ambition is to create a community of marketers working together to better understand and address the world's most critical problems.

A 'doing shop' rather than just a talking shop, MarketingKind began with 'online first' gatherings (provoked by COVID but a huge boost to our inclusiveness – we were bringing together members from five countries within weeks of going live). Our gatherings include Coffee with a Cause through which we 'upcycle' our marketing skills in support of good causes; Digital Fireside through which we coach each other in becoming more conscious leaders; and xChange through which we work on influencing the bigger stories that we live and work by to effect systems change. Month by month we involve some of the world's most recognised change-makers as well as grassroots pioneers in our activities and give our members a chance to work with their heroes, build an expanding portfolio of social and environmental achievements and enhance their own approach to purposeful leadership.

Just as running the matching platform is still a living laboratory of Collaborative Advantage, opening the virtual doors of MarketingKind has provided valuable first-hand insight into the demands of achieving a Purpose Upgrade in practice. Taking on meaningful local and global problems as 'briefs' has also given us a fair crack at offering the benefits of a Purpose Upgrade to the profession of marketing as a whole. After all, understanding the world's problems is essential to today's leaders, because we will only achieve meaningful and lasting outcomes by better addressing the deeper needs of the people we serve and on whom we depend.

Green Girls are doing it for themselves

MarketingKind's first 'Coffee with a Cause' was with Monique Ntumngia, a community-oriented problem-solver who has become one of Africa's leading young social entrepreneurs. It became apparent from listening to Monique that she herself had embodied the art of the Purpose Upgrade at a number of significant turning points in her life and the work of her organisation Green Girls.

Many of the most effective change-makers act on behalf of themselves and others like them. The suffragettes advocated for their own right to vote. The trade union movement was founded to enable mutual solidarity. Cooperatives are a mechanism for people to support themselves and each other. This is deeply connected to contextual insight. People best understand their own experience. It is also partly about conviction. People respond most powerfully to things they have lived. And it is partly about empowerment. People can best enable the actions of others in situations they are familiar with, because they know from the inside what they themselves can or have been able to do. They do not see themselves and each other as the passive recipients of support, but rather as active agents of their own change.

Monique has committed her life to the cause of female empowerment and the genesis of this came from her own childhood experiences. Monique's parents were from different tribes in Cameroon, and therefore following their marriage they were excluded from their own family gatherings. When she was twelve Monique lost her father, whose family subsequently took forcible possession of all his assets, throwing her and her mother on the street and threatening to kill them if they took legal action to reclaim what should have become their property. They went overnight from an affluent lifestyle to going without lights, potable water or access to other basic amenities. Monique considered changing her well-known family name, Ntumngia, because of the actions of her father's family, but she tells me that her mother advised her to keep it and to grow up to become a success so that one day she would have a strong reputation and her relatives would be ashamed of what they had done.

Monique made it to university, read law and went on to take a Master's in human rights. At twenty-two, she found herself in Nigeria as a policy officer in charge of gender and human rights, overseeing activity across the whole of West Africa. She advocated against female genital mutilation and other abuses of women, drawing on her personal experience of knowing what it is like to be deprived as a girl. She took far more personal risks than your average human rights lawyer and was not afraid of taking direct action when the legal process alone would be too slow to preserve lives. She has told me about learning parts of the Qur'an to infiltrate criminal communities motivated by a perversion of the Islamic faith, in a number of instances hiding women in the boots of cars to help them escape from community imprisonment. She has survived bomb blasts and was on the ground working to free women in Chibok when Boko Haram abducted one hundred girls, which you may recall from the global news headlines of the time.

As we saw in Chapter Three, many of the greatest change-makers are also in some sense accidental entrepreneurs. They witness a problem first-hand, realise a solution is needed and repurpose around that opportunity accordingly. Monique Ntumngia was in northern Nigeria in September 2014 with a grant and a team to support the education of young girls when one of the girls they were supporting approached her, saying, 'Madam, how can we study when we don't have light to read by?'. Monique realised that the real problem wasn't being solved. Substantial grants funded materials and textbooks but without light the girls couldn't study at night when they had time to learn. Girls spent their days collecting wood, cooking and maintaining dwellings and other domestic activity. The lack of contextual awareness among international donors meant that the funded materials were not specifically addressing the real nature of the challenge. Monique got together with her team and drafted a concept note to promote sustainable development with renewable energy. They repurposed their funding to purchase durable solar lamps so that girls without access to reliable electricity could still study.

Having reached 5,000 families with solar lamps across five states in Nigeria, Monique turned her attention back to Cameroon, which had an entirely different approach to energy. Cameroon has been affected more recently than Nigeria with electricity outages, but no development organisations were focused on the problem, nor was there any technology in widespread use to identify the right solutions for each tribal community, which depend on a variety of topographical factors from weather patterns to soil composition. Monique therefore devised a way to deploy AI and big data to unlock customised energy solutions for each community in support of the Sustainable Development Goals. By the end of 2016, the BBC discovered the activities of Monique and the Green Girls Organisation that she founded to implement her vision and broke the story. This led to substantial international coverage for her approach to training women in villages to generate biogas as their own renewable energy source to power their homes and, as a by-product, create valuable organic fertiliser. The women can then sell the fertiliser with a 30 per cent commission for Green Girls that funds the costs of their activities. The revenue from the sales often represents the totality of the income of the women earning it. Green Girls also finds markets for the women to sell the produce of their farms that the fertiliser helps them to grow. And in other communities Green Girls supports the creation of solar installations through sponsorship with local banks.

Despite her fearlessness with regards to her own safety, Monique has found it deeply distressing to hear about the suffering of others, especially from women who come to her in city environments in Cameroon who have been beaten by relatives or criminals, or who have fled violent or conflict-ridden areas. Realising that something needed to be done to support such micro-entrepreneurs in urban areas, and not just the rural communities already reached by the Green Girls, Monique got back together with her team. They considered simply providing grant assistance but realised this would quickly become unsustainable. Instead, they therefore decided to help the women coming to them to create their own micro-enterprises.

Once again, context was critical. Starting a business in Cameroon requires proof of at least 3,000 dollars of seed capital just for registration. There are many additional bureaucratic hurdles that can prevent people from being able to launch and grow their own enterprise, so Monique summoned her diplomatic skills to negotiate with a whole host of national and local authorities to gain special dispensations and forms of assistance for all women participating in a new Green Girls Entrepreneurial Hub. This enables them to start a business with as little as 50 dollars in funding and to be dispensed from an obligation to pay tax for their first two years of incorporation. Monique also stitched together a whole raft of partnerships to provide holistic support to each woman in context, addressing her psychological needs following the traumas she may have been through as well as the business skills and capabilities needed to run the new venture. She even arranges professional photo shoots for them and a package to enable them to create their own website to promote their services. The role of Green Girls changed thereby from delivering expertise to forging the shared narratives around which a whole raft of stakeholders can come together to bring about concerted change.

At the time of writing, the Hub is pioneering support for its first one hundred women, running businesses from making organic detergents to selling agricultural produce to offering administrative services such as virtual personal assistance to providing health and beauty services to city women. Typically, these micro-entrepreneurs have fled gender-based violence, are affected by disabilities or are in other ways suffering substantial exclusion. The Hub empowers them to establish their own sanctuary, turn their lives around and build a financially empowered future.

Monique ascribes her approach to seeing the wholeness of context wherever she works. She doesn't just see rural communities lacking electricity – she sees what happens to women and girls in the dark and what it takes to change the way communities organise themselves for lasting good. She doesn't just see women fleeing violence in cities, she sees the new lives they can be helped to build for themselves. She can trace her motivation all the way back to her own experiences as a twelve-year-old girl thrown from an affluent life to a life on the street with a conviction to turn life back around for the better and to empower others to achieve the same. She retains her sense of purpose always; but it is purpose on the move, rising to each new challenge as it presents itself, and not shying away from the underlying causes of the problems she tackles or their widespread ramifications.

> People just see there is no light but it goes so much deeper than that. It is a chain of problems. Women set out to fetch firewood. While they are out, they are sexually assaulted. They come back pregnant without even knowing it. They give birth at thirteen. They suffer fistula. They are excommunicated. If you do make it back okay [from fetching the firewood], you suffer from inhaling the smoke; it affects their vision, it harms their lungs and they get bronchitis.

Aid agencies can too often be focused on providing a fixed solution, but the problem with that is that a disconnect may emerge between the proposed solution and the real nature of the human problems that should be at the heart of the process. Targets reduce problems to their component parts and divorce them from lived experience. This reduces the effectiveness of interventions and makes them fragile in the face of change.

We need fewer fixed solutions bolted awkwardly onto dynamic problems and we need more people like Monique who can adapt around the needs of emerging problems and foster solutions that work across ecosystems and through communities as a whole, empowering greater outcomes from within than could ever be imposed from without. Communities flourish when women and girls are included, educated and empowered.

Can DSM (Dutch State Mines) transform into DSM (Do Something Meaningful)?

Repurposing may be great for entrepreneurs, it may come naturally to agile tech companies, it may help new players to sweep away incumbents, and it may be a perfect fit for community-building social innovators. But it simply can't work in many contexts, such as heavy industry. For example, there is no point in talking about purpose to a coal-mining business. The clue is in the name . . . But what if the very meaning of a name could change?

Royal DSM has embodied the art of repurposing in everything from the acronym that represents it to the core nature of its business and the total societal contribution that it makes. DSM originally stood for Dutch State Mines, and Royal DSM was indeed incorporated as a coal mining business in the Netherlands. But today the initials informally stand for 'Doing Something Meaningful', which quietly communicates a powerful capacity to repurpose from fundamentals while enlivening and adapting its values and culture.

The story is far from a case of purpose-washing for good PR. If it were just that, its leaders would have failed in their task, as DSM may be the biggest company that you've never heard of.

It has 23,000 employees worldwide, around 10 billion euros of annual revenue, a market capitalisation of around 35 billion euros and most of us have the chance to use their products every day, albeit often without realising it. It's worth digging into the heritage of the business to understand the fullness of its journey.

When DSM was created in 1902 coal-mining was a nationally vital line of business, and public good was baked into its state ownership structure. They dug coal out of the ground and provided it directly to people's homes for heating and illumination. DSM now has a long history during which it has endured two world wars, occupation by a foreign power and the Great Depression. Surviving such fierce challenges brings grit, resilience and adaptability and, as Hugh Welsh, President of DSM in North America tells me, 'these cultural hallmarks remain with the company today'. Changing times have obliged DSM to evolve significantly. 'While the coal is still there, the mines were closed by the state, so the option of remaining in the coal business was simply no longer available. DSM therefore initially moved into petrochemicals then industrial chemicals, which its leaders considered not so different a business from coal-mining, and which enabled them to use the capabilities they had in the company at the time.'

But ultimately DSM underwent a more revolutionary Purpose Upgrade. Feike Sijbesma became CEO of DSM in 2007. He knew about DSM's prior transition from coal-mining to industrial chemicals and concluded that there was a need for a further major transition. As a biologist, he grew up with an admiration for Charles Darwin, and he knew that it was not the biggest, fastest or strongest who survive but those who are the most adaptable. He was concerned by the tight and volatile margins in industrial chemicals, where DSM was easily dwarfed by its biggest global competitors who could therefore compete fiercely on price and where even new competitors from the Middle East had the advantage of cheaper access to raw materials. The market was also affected by a level of price volatility for which investors had a limited appetite. Most importantly, he didn't see how the chemicals products were truly meeting the future needs of society. He believed that finding opportunities to address the world's biggest problems would create more meaningful and purposeful work, better attract and engage employees and futureproof the business while also creating more stable margins. He therefore turned to the UN's Sustainable Development Goals and sought to identify business opportunities in food, nutrition, climate and the circular economy.

Feike knew that he couldn't make such a transition in one go. 'If you divest everything, you are left with an empty shell and a lot of money, not a company,' he explained to me. He also knew that there would be a need for experimentation and exploration to learn the new field, new competencies and organic growth as well as fresh acquisitions, explaining to his board that he envisioned a ten-to-fifteen-year journey to complete the change. That required buy-in not just from the board but right across the culture of the company, with a change of mindset from cost management in a legacy business to investing in innovation across whole new domains of activity.

Not all of DSM's investors were pleased with the new direction, and inevitably there were setbacks as well as progress. Paradoxically, Feike sought investors with a long-term focus but needed to communicate more frequently with them to take them on that journey. He also persuaded them to stick with DSM stock by promising reliable annual dividend payments even when the price of the shares went down as well as up. But the change paid off in the end. Since Feike took over as CEO, DSM shares have risen from 30 euros a share to over 200 euros per share today, representing a near seven-fold return on investment. And among many business accolades Feike also received the UN's Humanitarian of the Year award three years after taking over the leadership of the company. That is doing well by doing good.

The approach of beginning with the world's needs and working backwards from there permeates the business. As Hugh Welsh explains:

> Purpose at DSM begins not by looking inwards but by looking outwards. Decision-making starts by looking at the world and determining what the world's biggest challenges will be and then deciding whether the businesses in the portfolio are geared towards addressing at least some of those big global priorities. If they are not, then we divest those businesses. And if they are then we take the next step down. We first do the macro-analysis, then the portfolio analysis, then determine how we should deploy our capital. Do we have holes in the businesses that are working to solve some of the world's biggest problems that can be solved through acquisition or through our own research and development? And if so, where? And the next level down is our own operations. Are there ways we can improve our performance, financially, socially or environmentally? This might involve looking at initiatives ranging from investment in solar fields to programmes of employee engagement. Then we get to a more granular level, down to the types of people we seek to hire for those companies. It permeates the entire organisation and every layer of change it creates.

DSM spends its research and development investment in ways that align with its purpose. It nurtures a number of 'big bets', which are massive projects to bring new products and solutions to market that address some of the world's most pressing priorities. For example, DSM invented a feed ingredient that makes feed more digestible for cows and reduces cow methane emissions by more than 30 per cent, which is already having a significant impact in reducing greenhouse gas emissions from the agricultural sector. DSM also invested in an algo-fermentation plant that enables them to produce stevia at scale and make the previously expensive alternative to sugar far more universally available to contribute to alleviating the global obesity epidemic. And noting that carpet is the second biggest driver of landfill in the United States after diapers, the business pioneered the world's only fully recyclable carpet as well as a system for returning the used carpet at the end of its lifetime to be melted down into beadlets that are used in the manufacture of a new carpet as an excellent example of the circular economy in action while also avoiding the off-gassing of chemicals that are released from conventional latex carpets (though as far as I know, sadly DSM has never solved the problem of nappies).

Much of DSM's approach to purpose has been shaped by Feike's early experiences as CEO of the company. As a young leader he travelled to Davos for a World Economic Forum meeting during which he heard a female leader of an African country complain that Western donors send carbohydrate-based food in aid supplies that keeps people alive, but not nutritious food that could keep them truly productive, thereby arguably merely prolonging rather than alleviating the problems of poverty and malnutrition. As a result of this encounter, he felt compelled to develop a partnership with the United Nations World Food Programme, which has now improved the quality of the food delivered for more than 35 million people for more than a decade. What began as an intellectual pursuit for Feike at the World Economic Forum became personal through this relationship. He travelled to Bangladesh to see the programme in action. He listened to a mother ask him to take her child from her for fear that if he left the child there, it would not survive. This experience lives inside him to this day and he is clearly still moved as he tells the story.

Feike's career had progressed rapidly from early on, and he became CEO of DSM by the time he was forty-six. He recognised that leadership came with the responsibility to make sure that everyone he led was engaged in doing something worthwhile. While his MBA had taught him to maximise shareholder value, he saw the purpose of the economy not as to make money but to exchange goods and capabilities. 'The purpose of business', he tells me, 'is to help people lead happy lives together, not to make money; making money is a means to an end. Having those experiences in Africa made me question whether we are playing our role in the economy as we should do. I began to realise that you cannot be successful in a world that fails, nor even call yourself successful if you consider your responsibilities for our global village.' He did not want to look forward to a retirement in which he would talk only about shareholder value but one in which he could say to his grandchildren that as well as living well he did something to pass a better world on to them. More than that he realised that this didn't just go for him but for all the employees of DSM who also sought meaningful work.

Ultimately, Feike translated these experiences into the mission of the organisation, realising that for DSM to thrive for another hundred years, a catalytic narrative needed to be shared and lived by the next generation of leaders. DSM therefore works hard to replicate purposeful and transformative experiences for as many people as possible, so it is not just something that they are told but a story that they live for themselves. The company offers employees access to a programme called 'X-Time', whereby they can spend up to 10 per cent of their working time working on projects that may have little to do with their individual core function but give them an additional opportunity to make a difference aligned with DSM's greater purpose, which has been expressed as 'creating brighter lives **for all**'. This contributes to making work at DSM a vocation rather than just a job and stimulates a great deal of interest in working for the company.

DSM is also a founding member of a programme called Partners in Food Solutions to address long-term food needs in sub-Saharan Africa without depending on imported aid parcels. The Partners in Food Solutions programme empowers staff in its member businesses to connect remotely to local food producers on the ground in Africa to enhance their capabilities, be it in processing, food safety, marketing or other forms of technical support so that they can themselves create offerings that they can sell to the World Food Programme as well as through other donor programmes and commercial channels.

President Kagame spoke to DSM to explain that his population in Rwanda had the highest percentage of stunted growth in all of sub-Saharan Africa. Any investment he could make in infrastructure would mean nothing if the children of Rwanda could not reach their potential due to malnutrition. In response, DSM decided to build a food manufacturing plant in Kigali. So, together with non-traditional partners including the Centers for Disease Control, the UK Development Bank, the development bank FMO in the Netherlands and the International Finance Corporation (the development arm of the World Bank), DSM built African Improved Foods for

Rwanda. It produces a fortified porridge that is sold to the World Food Programme, the government of Rwanda and the public market. The porridge is sold for profit to make the operation truly sustainable, employing 400 Rwandans in the plant, sourcing all the raw ingredients locally from small-holder farmers to boost Rwandan agriculture while feeding over 2.5 million children.

For many of the farmers who participate, this is the first time they have ever produced to a contract, which means that for the first time they can also access loans to invest in better equipment and greater productivity and make the transition from subsistence farming to running a viable business.

DSM intends to replicate this numerous times across Africa, with the goal of eliminating hunger and fostering a system of local sourcing, local production for local people and ultimately even local ownership.

The transformative experience of working to support these programmes is matched by the purposeful nature of the core business. Employees that work for DSM, whether in a function such as legal, communications or human resources, working on a production floor or working in research and development can all tie the core work they are doing back to something meaningful that is going on in the world.

Hugh talks about one particular day that brings to life what DSM and its purpose means to him: the day Hurricane Sandy hit. Hugh was in the New Jersey office and had just signed the $660 million acquisition of Fortitech. He had been in his office working all night and into the next day when he finally opened the door in the morning and, to his surprise, there was no one there in a building that by then should have had five hundred people back in it. After turning on the news and discovering what was happening, he called his father, who first advised him to get their crisis management manual which Hugh went and retrieved, then promptly told him to 'throw it away', concluding that, 'It's simple. You take care of your people and they will take care of the business.'

Hugh realised the building had power, heat, food and working showers while nowhere else did. DSM even had its own gym. He therefore invited all his staff to bring their families to the building and stay as long as they needed. And without any word from him, the staff spontaneously got their laptops up and running in conference rooms and never missed a beat. Accounts payable, payroll and all essential business activities were completed in the middle of one of the biggest natural disasters to ever hit New Jersey. Years later when Hurricane Florence was bearing down on North and South Carolina, DSM staff volunteered to man the plant and maintain its safety while employees with family members to protect could return home to take care of them. And not a single customer even failed to receive their product.

But even a business the size of DSM cannot bring about change alone. It must therefore forge shared purpose with its stakeholders outside as well as inside the business. As Hugh comments, 'We break down our strategy into improving our own operations, enabling external stakeholders and advocating for change.' DSM's advocacy includes a whole range of issues from climate change to gun control that use its influence to drive positive change regardless of whether that in turn drives the bottom line. 'Changing the stories that we live and work by is a broader part of being a healthy business in a healthy society,' Hugh adds. Indeed, Hugh was largely responsible for convincing the US Chambers of Commerce to acknowledge for the first time that climate change was man-made and a priority for business to address.

Serving a greater purpose inevitably changes how success must be measured. As Hugh concludes:

> It is no longer practical or proper to exclusively serve shareholder value. Looking at issues like climate change, you would not take decisions to build solar fields at your manufacturing plants or switch to full use of renewable electricity if your sole purpose was to maximise shareholder value in the near term. Upgrading the purpose of an enterprise involves creating benefits for all stakeholders, with management boards that take a holistic approach to understanding the needs of the constituents they serve, with shareholders being one group alongside employees, communities and customers. The decisions that are made are for the collective benefit of all of them. Over the long run there is more alignment among stakeholders than there are differences. Each group can only prosper when they all prosper.

DSM is also ahead of industry in the public-company space and beyond in tying purpose to compensation, which began with Feike's and the managing board's own remuneration when he was CEO. 'I realised after three or four years into my journey that my remuneration was based only on financial criteria and that this was wrong and did not match the story I was telling about the purpose of the company,' he told me. The board was initially, in Feike's words, 'a bit distant' to his proposal to base his remuneration half on non-financial criteria including sustainability targets because no global business was doing that at the time, but he talked them round and then rolled the approach out across the rest of the business. This was so radical that it made the front page of the *Financial Times*. Since then, any leaders joining the company and listening to a CSR talk thinking that they've heard it all before have had a wake-up call on discovering that half of their short-term bonus and half of their long-term stock options would be tied not to financial performance but to targets such as employee engagement, reduction in greenhouse gas emissions, energy efficiency and an even more sustainable portfolio of solutions.

Learning to repurpose often comes from adversity. The culture of DSM hasn't been roses and champagne throughout its history. Hugh first came to the company shortly after the business acquired Hoffmann La Roche's vitamins business. One part of DSM was therefore a relatively anonymous old chemical company, and another a newly owned former part of a global business with a strong brand. Each group had a grudge to bear. The former because they felt they were being pushed out of the company and the latter because they had left a Swiss business with a heritage that they were proud of for a Dutch one they knew little about. They lacked a shared purpose or common experience to bring them together. Then came the financial crisis of 2008. This meant that DSM had to face one of the biggest challenges in the company's history in the heart of one of the biggest challenges of recent decades to confront the global economy. But through that period, instead of going through wholesale reductions in staffing or employee benefits, DSM stayed the course and its leaders communicated with staff every day to reassure them that the business was investing in them. Not cutting staff despite such an uncertain environment turned employee engagement around and gave each employee a deeper sense that the purpose of the business was real and that they, as its people, were the most important asset of the business.

When Feike handed over the CEO-ship in 2020, he was named as DSM's Honorary Chair. Fitting with the culture of DSM that values action over ego, rather than appoint a single

CEO, DSM appointed a duo as Feike's successors: Geraldine Matchett, the former CFO, and Dimitri de Vreeze, who had been a managing board member for some time. The pair have since shared the responsibility of leadership as co-CEOs.

Within a few weeks of taking on their new roles, Geraldine and Dimitri were faced with the pandemic and could perhaps have been forgiven for playing it safe. Instead, they sought to make a greater contribution to society and build an even more thriving enterprise than ever before. While I have been writing this book, Geraldine and Dimitri have been leading perhaps the most extensive Purpose Upgrade in the history of the company.

As Geraldine explains to me:

> It helped that we were not starting from scratch. Dimitri and I had both come from within DSM and have between us lived its values over many years. There was a lot of firefighting to do with the sudden arrival of the pandemic after only our first roadshow, but on the other hand a crisis can be when your values most stand out. Our colleagues worked hard on how they could not just keep the business running but support their communities, and we began to manufacture products that were not at all our line of business, such as masks, swabs and sanitiser just because we could and they were needed. But more fundamentally we worked throughout the pandemic on our mindset as a business, spreading a caring, collaborative and courageous culture through conversations and exchanges between our colleagues across the company.

While purpose-level change required the right internal culture, it was not a culture of looking inwards but rather of looking outwards at the world's needs. Geraldine, Dimitri and their colleagues cast their eyes firmly on the broken state of the global food system. They found the system to be failing in terms of its contribution to human health, the health of the planet, and the livelihoods of people who work the land. Dimitri cites World Food Programme statistics as thoughtfully as any NGO leader. One in ten people suffer from malnutrition, and hunger rose by 15 per cent last year, while at the same time one in four people is overweight, and poor-quality nutrition is a major driver of illness and disease. Two billion people are micro-nutrient deficient, while food systems are the second biggest cause of the climate emergency and are also themselves put at risk by the droughts, floods and fires that it is causing. Food also drives deforestation and 30 per cent of food is wasted, while half of the world's one billion farmers live in poverty.

I put it to Geraldine that changing the global food system is a contentious issue; that food activists want to see local, seasonal, varied food, not monoculture crops, and that big business is often seen as the problem not the solution, as it often makes us more and more dependent on an increasingly fragile and destructive global trade. She responded by first telling me that before going into business she had studied sustainable development at Cambridge University and could just as easily have been drawn to working at Greenpeace, but chose to work in business because, whereas at one time religion was a predominant influence on society, followed later by national governments, today it is global business that drives our interconnected systems. 'If you want to change the world for the better,' she argues, 'the private sector offers you perhaps the most valuable lever to pull.' She went on to explain that fixing the food system requires us to diminish the harm caused by existing large-scale production as well as supporting new alternatives. DSM is taking the 'both end' approach to fostering the emergence of breakthrough solutions such as plant-based alternative proteins while also recognising that people will continue to choose animal-based proteins for some time to come so she is also working on bringing radical reductions to the environmental harm caused by meat and dairy production.

A similar ideological pragmatism extends into improving human health:

> We also know that today, only a small minority of people have access to an ideal diet. So we are working on fortified foods for low-income countries that overcome the challenges of micro-nutrient deficiency while also developing technologies that enable much more personalised nutrition based on your DNA, your individual needs, your level of activity and the season of the year, to make it more affordable, accessible and sustainable to get all the nutrients you need.

As a geographer, Geraldine is at home discussing how to maintain fertile topsoil conditions and the practical challenges faced by farmers in some of the poorest parts of the world, for whom DSM is able to provide long-term contracts that enable them to invest in developing practical sustainable practices such as the cob model of storing and drying crops to avoid mould contamination and the associated waste that too often comes from farming in conditions of extreme poverty.

She cites five food system commitments for which DSM will be independently audited and that demonstrate its capacity to bring a Purpose Upgrade to whole systems of food production. DSM pledges by 2030 to close the micro-nutrient gap of 800 million vulnerable people; support the immunity of half a billion people; enable double-digit farm emissions reduction; reach 150 million people with nutritious plant-based foods; and support the livelihoods of 500,000 smallholder farmers. That's a true Wealth of Change.

'If you have the capability to drive change, then you have the responsibility to make it happen,' Dimitri maintains. The commitment of the co-CEOs to making this work is reflected in a substantial re-organisation of the company to orientate it around a clearer purpose than ever before. DSM is now structured in three business groups that all relate to addressing the food system through more sustainable farming, keeping the world's growing population healthy and providing nutritious and sustainable foods respectively. That extra level of focus will help DSM not only keep up with change but accelerate its leadership role in driving change across the food system. It will make the difference that DSM can make more salient and accountable. And while it also brings with it the need to divest its valuable materials business, DSM makes even divestment purposeful; the materials business is a valuable operation and it is believed that its staff will be able to pursue an even brighter future with a new ownership able to offer the right focus to bring its potential to greater fruition. This is not empty posturing but a model that has already been proved successful in the past; the recycled carpet solution that we encountered earlier in this story is now making a bigger difference than ever under a new owner for whom the product is not a sideline but a star offering.

I put it to Dimitri that when authors write books on corporate purpose, a small number of well-known examples are regularly cited. DSM by contrast is a hidden gem, perhaps because as a predominantly B2B enterprise it has less consumer recognition than, say, a Patagonia or a Whole Foods Market. In some ways this enables DSM to tackle grittier problems than consumer-facing brands, some of which can end up focusing on what looks good rather than what unlocks the greatest change. As Inge Massen-Biemans, Vice-President of Corporate Affairs, tells me, 'If you don't get stuck into the problem it's hard to be part of the solution.' DSM's B2B approach also brings with it a different approach to scale. As both Geraldine and Dimitri reveal, DSM's solutions can increase the sustainability of whole sectors and are not limited to individual brands. In the case of DSM's methane-reducing solutions, for example, it was hard at first to get into individual supply chains because the product disrupted existing business models. DSM had to work to foster an operating environment that placed a higher value on reducing food system emissions, changing the priorities and practices of an entire sector.

The work of repurposing is, however, never finished. One challenge on the horizon that Hugh warns us to pay attention to is that huge layers of middle management across industry will be made obsolete very soon as a consequence of AI and machine learning. Roles such as aggregating data, preparing reports, setting key performance indicators,[3] aggregating metrics and reporting up will be replaced at an accelerating rate by intuitive DRP[4] systems in companies. As Hugh concedes, 'If we don't find a way to handle that not insignificant portion of the workforce whose jobs will be replaced by technology, then we'll be putting ourselves not just as a company but as a society in a very awkward position in the not-too-distant future.' Indeed, coronavirus has already proven to be a catalyst for change in many businesses, because management has learned that they didn't need as many people as they thought and that technology can do a lot of the work that they previously thought only people could do.

Hugh says:

We need to start looking at employees as lifelong learners and support our people in constantly up-skilling in their own roles and functions as well as acquiring the capacity to move into new roles and functions as the ones that they have today become obsolete. My head of communications was previously in human resources, but her role disappeared when many HR processes became automated. Similarly, many legal and paralegal roles became redundant when AI could draft simple contracts more effectively, but rather than end people's employment, we found other roles for them to play within the company. Retraining begins while people are in their old job. People are smart and can tell when their roles are going to become unnecessary. But we go to people and say, while you are in your current job you can train for a new one. This keeps folks very much engaged in both roles.

The example set by DSM has a wide relevance to today's challenges. In making the transition from coal-mining, a once respectable but now problematic endeavour, ultimately to tackling the climate emergency and the broken food system, DSM is a powerful metaphor for the kinds of Purpose Upgrade that are most needed across the economy and society as we transition from one phase of development to the next.

As Hugh concludes, '"Doing Something Meaningful" is for everyone. If you are not doing something meaningful, find something else to do.'

We'll turn to a systematic way to implement a Purpose Upgrade in your enterprise next.

For your enterprise

- How has your organisation evolved over time and when has the drive to repurpose been felt most strongly?
- Where has leadership come from or failed to come from? What has been most necessary to enable change to spread across the organisation and its stakeholders and to what degree has this been successful?
- What are the costs of failing to repurpose today? And what could now be the opportunities for achieving a Purpose Upgrade?

Chapter Seven

YOUR PURPOSE UPGRADE

A Purpose Upgrade can redefine the problems that we address, the solutions that we create and the outcomes that we achieve through an enterprise. It can drive change at every scale of activity, from the mission of the organisation as a whole down to the tasks completed each day within it by every member of staff and to all points of contact with its stakeholders.

More importantly, through the influence of the enterprise's activity, a Purpose Upgrade can play a part in elevating change in the world outside its boundaries, empowering its customers to enhance their lives, communities to become more vibrant, partners to co-create the future, and investors to build long-term societal and economic value.

A Purpose Upgrade can be implemented across an enterprise in response to major changes in the internal or external environment of material concern to a business, as well as periodically in line with planning cycles and regular reviews.

A mini-Purpose Upgrade can also be deployed specifically to redirect any particular activity within an enterprise to increase the value that it unlocks.

The potential for a **Purpose Upgrade** is always available and can never be exhausted. Our changing world requires us to be ever vigilant in maintaining the situational intelligence and adaptability needed to further repurpose and revitalise our activity whenever this is necessary or useful.

Purpose mythbusting

As we have seen, a number of commonly cited half-truths exist with regards to the purpose of enterprise that are worth re-evaluating so that they do not hold us back when we apply a Purpose Upgrade in practice. They may be found in the following claims:

1) **'Purpose is our North Star.'** This concept has the merit of indicating that purpose can serve as an important guide. However, while the North Star is inanimate and eternally fixed, the purpose of enterprise, like human purpose, needs to live and adapt in changing circumstances. If Royal DSM treated its purpose as a North Star, it would still be digging coal out of the ground and certainly would not be working to achieve the United Nations' Sustainable Development Goals. It is better to acknowledge that while our current purpose can help us to chart our path to the future, new possibilities for greater aspiration will reveal themselves along the way. Work on purpose is never finished, because it is a means through which we create the new in a changing world.

2) **'Purpose is about authenticity.'** This concept also has merit in highlighting that we cannot legitimately claim a purpose that is at odds with our decisions, actions and capabilities. But it also limits us by suggesting that purpose may come from

introspection alone and 'just being ourselves' no matter what. A better way of thinking about purpose is to realise that purpose is a product of the relationship between ourselves and others in context. We find and fulfil our purpose with and through each other according to the situations that present themselves. The same is true in enterprise. A purpose of providing 'authentic' gastronomic delight is pointless in an environment of food poverty.

3) **'Purpose is single-minded.'** This observation highlights the focus that purpose brings. Purpose is indeed as much about what we don't do as about what we do. However, in an enterprise environment, work on purpose must integrate many interests across the stakeholders of an enterprise, all of whom must thrive for the business to succeed. It is more about aligning aspirations, interests and benefits than just sticking to our own pre-conceived notions. We must also never lose our peripheral vision, lest our current purpose blind us to future possibilities or necessities. We must not let the lens of our focus become the blinker of our ignorance.

The Purpose Upgrade as a new art of enterprise success

The most powerful way to redirect a business is to improve its definition of what success looks like. And yet the purpose of business can be one of the most difficult things to challenge because it is often so deeply embedded in our assumptions that it lies out of the domain of discussion as if it were unquestionable.

We can overcome this by applying the lens of a Purpose Upgrade to bring intentional improvement across an enterprise as well as to individual activities within it.

As we saw in the Introduction, businesses have a long history of learning to adapt to change in progressively more ambitious ways. Where business had its origins in mechanisms of simple exchange, the increasing sophistication of markets led to innovation and changes in what businesses offer. This began with incremental innovation that made existing offerings better: better tasting, better looking, better functioning, etc. We learned to be more ambitious with our innovation by combining elements from different domains through discontinuous or recombinant innovation, from putting wheels on suitcases (which was rejected as a concept by the world's leading suitcase manufacturers of its day!) to the now iconic three devices in one – a phone, a music player and a web browser – Steve Jobs' iPhone.

After at least many decades of practising the art of innovation, we progressed to a greater level of ambition with the arrival of the Internet and associated communications technologies. These changed not just what we offer, but how we offer it. Businesses have adopted processes of digital transformation, opening every facet of business activity up to the demands and opportunities of ubiquitous connectivity.

Our global ecology is becoming ever-more impinging as a contiguous whole, brought together and made more dynamic but also more vulnerable by its internal relationships. The changes in humankind's needs as we face ever greater interconnectedness and interdependence now require us to move beyond changes in what we offer and how we offer it to a more frequent evaluation of the purpose that we should pursue in the first place.

Businesses set in motion ripple effects of consequence that reach right across society and are in turn impacted by the health and prosperity of the society in which they operate. Ethical considerations, existential risk and the changing expectations of all stakeholders therefore add a powerful new dimension to the need to integrate a fuller situational awareness than businesses may previously have developed in determining their purpose, aspiration and goals.

Purpose in enterprise must be outward-looking to involve all stakeholders in collective change. The leaders of a business cannot limit their thinking on purpose to their own interests or to the internal capabilities of their enterprise. Customers do not just receive value, but actively create it. And they must judge that they can create more value from using a business's products and services than it costs to use them, or they won't become customers in the first place. Purpose must drive demand by tying into the goals and intentions of the people we serve, and choosing which customer purposes to fulfil is key to any Purpose Upgrade.

Similarly, colleagues create the value that an enterprise delivers through their discretionary efforts and creativity, not just through the instructions that they receive from their managers; communities provide the setting in which commerce can take place and their level of vibrancy creates the conditions for success or failure; partners provide the complementary offerings that enterprises and their stakeholders depend upon, and their active engagement shapes shared possibilities; and investors make the commitment to the future that enables enterprise activity to take place at all. These relationships can only work in the long term if they involve all stakeholders in the active pursuit of worthwhile purpose and mutual reward.

Business advantage therefore accrues from developing expertise in an understanding of human purpose and how people make sense of their social and physical environment, find ways to improve their conditions and take action to bring about the changes they desire. This means understanding people in context, working with their aspirations and empowering actions that they choose for themselves.

A Purpose Upgrade provides a focal point through which we can elevate positive reciprocal change through our enterprise relationships, defining our purpose with and through the aspirations of the stakeholders whom we can best empower and who make the biggest difference to our success.

Preparing for a Purpose Upgrade

Our stakeholders live and work in environments of change. To meet their needs we must therefore foster a living purpose.

Achieving this depends on our ability to understand our State of Emergence and the changing situations that we find ourselves in. Our purpose may be born of the problems that we choose to solve.

The key to finding better problems to solve is in understanding the challenges that we address in context. We can foster greater contextual thinking as the first dimension of a Purpose Upgrade by applying the Five Contextual Shifts framework of Chapter Three as well as addressing the questions for reflection at the end of that chapter.

Living purpose relies on identifying the right ways to solve the problems that we choose to address. This comprises the actions that we undertake as well as the actions that we enable our stakeholders to undertake in response to them. It reveals the path that we travel and is described in the stories that we live and work by.

The key to achieving a better response to our problems therefore lies in identifying greater narratives of collective change to direct it, revealing a Garden of Forking Paths through which we and our stakeholders can move away from negative change and towards positive change. We can co-create the narratives that guide our responses and influence the actions of our stakeholders as the second dimension of a Purpose Upgrade, by applying the Six Narrative Drivers framework from Chapter Four as well as addressing the questions for reflection at the end of that chapter.

Living purpose also requires us to be able to envisage a future of positive outcomes. This identifies the goals we should aim for, the results that we should seek to achieve and the rewards that we can share and enjoy.

This requires us to achieve more inclusive change as the third dimension of a Purpose Upgrade to actively inspire and involve our stakeholders in achieving financial and non-financial benefits together. We can define our Wealth of Change as the overall difference that we make in the world and make it more compelling by applying the Stakeholder Dividends framework from Chapter Five, as well as by addressing the reflections at the end of that chapter.

We have seen that a fourth dimension makes these first three possible and maintains their dynamic health: the capacity for renewal.

We can foster the art of renewal as the fourth dimension of a Purpose Upgrade by applying the reflections found at the end of each chapter of this book and by maintaining a stance of openness to elevating our purpose when the context in which we operate requires this.

Adaptive change maintains the fit between our activities and the environment in which we operate. This adjusts our cycle of change into an upwards spiral of progress.

Maladaptive change or stasis on the other hand leads to an ever-greater disconnection between our activities and the environment in which we operate, leading to a downwards spiral of decline.

The scope of a Purpose Upgrade

The opportunity for a Purpose Upgrade exists in every aspect of change that we control within an enterprise or influence in the world outside its boundaries.

We can apply the analysis from the Five Contextual Shifts, Six Shared Narratives and Stakeholder Dividends frameworks to whichever level of activity we are reviewing. A Purpose Upgrade can focus on a specific initiative such as a new partnership, product, service or acquisition. Or it can be applied across an enterprise as a whole. In each case it is a question of framing the boundaries of analysis around the scope of change considered.

A Purpose Upgrade must ultimately involve all relevant stakeholders in the change that it creates for the biggest differences to be achieved.

Organising a Purpose Upgrade

We can describe a Purpose Upgrade as an always-available event at every level of enterprise activity and engagement.

It is 'always available' because we can never identify the ultimate absolute greatest purpose to pursue; nor can we perfectly align the entirety of any action with that purpose. Each new moment that passes can reveal ways to further optimise our purpose and how we can best pursue it in the light of fresh emergence.

But it is also an 'event' because it represents a distinct, identifiable and consequential change in our intentionality. We must therefore use our judgement in deciding when to commit to a

Purpose Upgrade. Typically, it makes sense to review the purpose of our enterprise and the purpose of activities and programmes within it both on a regular, periodic basis, such as in alignment with existing planning and review cycles and also in the light of specific fresh challenges and opportunities that may impinge upon us as they emerge, such as the approach of a major societal or industry change, crisis or tipping point. If a Purpose Upgrade has not previously been deployed in an enterprise, the right timing is almost certainly now. Cognitive biases most commonly lead to underestimating rather than overestimating the urgency of the need for a Purpose Upgrade, because it takes less effort to imagine a continuation of the past than the arrival or creation of an alternative future. As Feike Sijbesma has told me:

> Too many companies, in my view, wait too long until the need for change becomes so pressing that you don't have time to do it in an orderly way. My advice is do it on time, before you are in financial stress, otherwise you won't have the freedom to change from the inside, but change will be imposed upon you. Some people find it hard to lift their anchor while they can still fish, but if you want to fish in another part of the ocean you have to lift your anchor even if it feels dangerous or scary.

When reviewing the purpose of an enterprise as a whole, it often makes sense to involve an independent source of guidance and facilitation, the better to reveal hidden assumptions, create a safe space for open conversation and overcome groupthink. It is not usually best achieved, however, by 'outsourcing' the work as a whole to an external firm. Living through the process of establishing a Purpose Upgrade is key to understanding, taking responsibility for and delivering on its benefits. It also makes sense to involve external participants from across the stakeholder base of the enterprise, to better understand and integrate their perceptions, to unlock the potential for mutual commitment and to access an external 'reality check' on new propositions. A successful Purpose Upgrade depends upon stitching together many acts of stakeholder cooperation and must motivate and enable the self-directed activity of external stakeholders as a key part of its success.

It can be useful to establish a board committee to oversee an enterprise-wide Purpose Upgrade and to monitor enterprise purpose over time to ensure that alignment is maintained between all dimensions of an enterprise and the evolving understanding of purpose. The work of a Purpose Upgrade typically begins with a core champion or group of champions and can spiral outwards to involve progressively more colleagues and external stakeholders as it is developed.

As well as participating in each Purpose Upgrade through their own insights and according to their own role, each employee should be given access to a living set of statements of enterprise purpose and empowered to relate their own planning, responsibilities, priorities and professional development to that purpose as well as to identify the potential for further purpose-level adaptation when needed. Thinking about purpose and acting on it must become an everyday priority.

An enterprise-wide Purpose Upgrade

Once you have prepared the way by applying the Five Contextual Shifts, Six Shared Narratives and Five Stakeholder Dividends frameworks as well as the reflections throughout the book, a Purpose Upgrade may be deployed across an enterprise as a whole.

Upgrade your values

The primary problem with capitalism, as identified by former governor of the Bank of England Mark Carney, is that we have come to subjugate values to value, forgetting that value is built on values.[1] The economy and the businesses within it must serve society, not the other way around. This is a problem ripe for solving through a Purpose Upgrade.

As Aristotle observed, we become just by performing just acts; temperate by performing temperate acts; brave by performing brave acts.

Values are the fundamental rules by which we judge one thing more important than another. They are the currency of our decision-making. We may attempt to express them in our statements of purpose, but, more than that, we show them through the implicit priorities revealed by our actions. What values would your customers or other people who come into contact with the business attribute to you?

Proponents of a static North Star approach to purpose might argue that you can't upgrade your values. To admit change to your core values is to betray your own principles. The whole point of values is that they remain unchanging.

And yet.

While changing our values every day would lead to chaos, not stopping to reflect periodically and when needed on how we can upgrade them is to cease to grow. How have your values changed since you were a teenager? What would you expect them to be by the time you look back on your life as a whole? The living personal growth we undertake as individuals finds its counterpart in organisations that recognise that their fundamental values must come to life in an environment that is changing and through people who are not finished. We adapt our values according to

215

our circumstances, and the nature of our work in turn brings further change to those circumstances.[2] Access to greater autonomy, for example, will likely increase the degree to which we come to value independence of thought.

Values must become specific. Rarely in current practice are values sufficiently tied to the value creation process, and this can deprive the values of a business of their greatest meaning. It's as if the two uses of the word 'value' have no connection. If your values statements could live equally happily in a business that serves a completely different purpose, the chances are that your concept of values is not particular enough to make a difference to strategy, innovation, engagement and decision-making throughout the enterprise. The Zappos core value of creating 'fun and a little weirdness'[3] that empowers staff to let their inner quirkiness shine would not fit well with the consulting firm Deloitte, for example, and that is a good thing for *both* companies.

Values must also be challenging. If they are easy to own, they are easy to imitate. If they don't stretch you to discomfort, they don't bring out your best. If they are too easy to sign off on, they may not be worth signing up for.

Which values do you work by? What defining moments have best brought this to life so far? How can they be expressed? How can your stakeholders trust you to live up to them? And what opportunities are there to revisit them?

Upgrade your vision

Many so-called vision statements comprise a vision of the organisation and what it will become. While such an inward-looking vision may be useful for colleagues and investors, it is unlikely to fully mobilise external stakeholder engagement.

An outward-looking vision, however, describes the world in a desirable future state that gives stakeholders a reason to support the business and to root for its success. For an international development NGO, such a vision might be defined in terms of a world in which poverty is eradicated; for a bank operating in developing economies, it might be a world in which no one is excluded from the benefits of financial services; for a cultural attraction, it might be thought of in terms of a local community in which every family has access to a world of creativity. For the German pharmaceutical business Bayer, the vision is a world of 'Health for all, hunger for none'.[4]

How will the world be changed by your work? What problems will be overcome? How will lives be lived differently? How will communities be strengthened? And how will partners and investors thrive?

Your vision is your intended future legacy. It may be encoded in words, but its ultimate embodiment lives in the people whom you serve and the change they are able to create thanks to your support. It can also be fractional. Each part of an enterprise may be responsible for a part of the enterprise vision, and each employee can be supported in fostering a vision of the changes to people's lives that they most wish to unlock within that. Many people have enjoyed the popular legend that when John F. Kennedy toured the NASA headquarters in 1961 and asked a janitor why he was working so late, the janitor responded, 'Mr President, I'm helping put a man on the moon.'

Your vision can be upgraded when there is a need or opportunity to change your ambition to create a different set of end-outcomes in the world. This may come about due to change in the external environment; uncovering a fresh perspective from within the enterprise; or as part of a scheduled review process.

It may even come about because your prior vision has been completely achieved.

Your vision of a better world makes your work relevant to the people you serve and adds external legitimacy to the actions you pursue. It pulls your stakeholders forwards towards a future promise that you can fulfil and a set of aspirations that they can achieve.

Upgrade your mission

Your mission is the role you play in the world. It is the challenge you undertake. It is the action for which you are responsible. Every enterprise and every employee within an enterprise either has a mission to pursue or is left without a contribution to make. Well-known mission statements include:

- Tesla: Accelerate the world's transition to sustainable energy.[5]
- Timberland: Equip people to make a difference in the world.[6]
- IKEA: Create a better everyday life for the many.[7]

A clear mission means that fewer prescriptive rules are needed to second-guess every eventuality. This can liberate colleagues to act congruously according to the context of each situation that they encounter using their own best judgement. It overcomes the 'computer says no' mindset that can hold bureaucratic organisations back and liberates the greater talent and discretionary efforts of employees.

While we cannot fully ensure our vision, because its fulfilment depends on the voluntary participation of our stakeholders, our mission is our responsibility to deliver.

We owe it to ourselves to make our mission exciting to us. If it doesn't get us out of bed in the morning, it leaves us vulnerable to being overtaken by the habits formed by yesterday's outdated assumptions and to a slow (or rapid) period of decline.

As with our vision, our mission can be fractional. Each business group or other part of an enterprise may have its own segment of the enterprise mission. And each colleague can be empowered to write their own mission statement which relates their own activity to the mission of the enterprise.

In an environment of change, we must keep our quest eternally renewed. How is the world changing? How does this affect our stakeholders? What is the greater difference that we can make today? And how can we use this to upgrade our mission over time?

Upgrade your strategy

A strategy turns a purpose into a plan of action that connects the capabilities of a business with external opportunities.

Working with purpose elevates what would otherwise be an assessment of reductive and transactional *market opportunities* into the evaluation of greater *opportunities for positive societal change*. Such an assessment means that the kinds of opportunities considered for an enterprise in the first place are rooted in a spirit of contribution. They are more likely to be genuinely useful to stakeholders and are therefore also likely to be a source of greater long-term profitability.

Similarly, working with purpose elevates what would otherwise be an *assessment of internal capabilities* to an evaluation of the greater *unique role* for the enterprise to play in unlocking societal change. This transcends traditional analysis of strength relative to competitors and opens the door to identifying missing gaps that an enterprise can use its capabilities to address

219

that provide either a true alternative or a complement to existing offerings. Netflix, for example, is well known for the belief that its most significant competitor is sleep. The most valuable strategies identify a role to play in people's lives that would be missed if it was taken away.

A strong strategy fulfils an attractive opportunity for societal change with a unique role for the enterprise to play. Its relationship with purpose is iterative. Purpose creates a territory in which to develop strategy; but strategy can also help us identify a useful territory for purpose to demarcate. This further reveals why creative development and iteration are vital tools for work on purpose. A Purpose Upgrade is always chosen explicitly or implicitly from a broader range of available options.

Upgrade your operations

A Purpose Upgrade may involve redirecting existing capabilities or developing new ones. As a rule of thumb, opportunities earlier in the following sequence are most commonly easier to achieve because they involve less change, while those later in the sequence are usually more difficult but also potentially even more impactful because they involve greater change.

1 We can upgrade existing capabilities to better align them with their current purpose, such as by redirecting service delivery to better achieve an existing goal.
2 We can extend or enhance existing capabilities, for example through training or innovation to enable a greater goal to be reached.
3 We can repurpose existing activities to a new end, such as using existing assembly lines to produce alternative product offerings.

4 We can develop new capabilities through investment, such as by working with new technology to fulfil a new purpose altogether.

5 We can purchase new capabilities through acquisition, such as by adding to the portfolio of businesses within a group to fulfil a new and previously unachievable purpose.

We can also adapt our operational capability through external collaboration. A Purpose Upgrade may change our relationship with existing partners or lead us to form new partnerships to access new capabilities without the need to bring those capabilities in-house. We can further increase our capabilities through collective action across externally led industry and multi-stakeholder groups. As Geraldine Matchett, co-CEO of DSM, put it to me, 'Asking what we can do together that we cannot do alone is often a powerful way to solve more ambitious problems.'

Upgrade your brand

For many businesses, brand equity is their most valuable asset. And yet arguably it is not owned by the business at all.

Your brand is a signpost used by your stakeholders to find their way to the fulfilment of their purpose. It is a storehouse of their trust in you.

A brand can be upgraded for external audiences by strengthening the visual and written cues that make it recognisable and compelling, and better aligning them with new purpose.

A brand can also be upgraded for internal audiences through its better use as a filtering lens through which to discriminate between actions and behaviours that live up to your mission and those that fall outside or beneath it. A brand creates your identity by shaping the actions that you repeatedly take and defining the business that you therefore become.

Brands may also be fractional. A corporate brand may provide the backdrop against which a product brand, portfolio of product brands or even set of businesses or business groups with their own portfolios may be presented. While the degree of alignment and integration may vary from situation to situation, it is important to avoid entanglement through which these brands actively work against their respective purposes, such as arguably happened when Unilever's Axe/Lynx brand promoted a form of laddish thinking that may have been in conflict with the vision of the empowerment of women in thinking differently about beauty championed by the business's Dove brand. Axe's marketing has since been redirected to avoid this clash.

Upgrade your value propositions

Our value propositions present the individual benefits that our enterprise can offer. These propositions encode our promises and make us predictable in ways that we invite people to trust. A value proposition is not necessarily a guarantee: but it is a sincere pledge to do our best in living up to our claims.

Each proposition contains its own dimensions of purpose. Who is this for? What is this for? And why does it make a difference? These purpose-level foundations are not set in stone forever. Nor should they be, because that would inhibit our learning and growth. In the case of almost every innovation, we learn as we go to tune into the right customers and meet their most valuable needs as they become progressively more visible to us.

However ambitious we are to create change, we best begin by meeting the present needs of our most accessible and engaged stakeholders. We must therefore ask: Who are they?

What does 'better' look like for them? What promise will engage them in choosing us on the journey to their goals? We need these early adopters to help us learn how best to deliver change and also reach a broader base of customers and stakeholders through their influence.

As we expand to move beyond these pioneers, our purpose must evolve to reflect the priorities of this broader group. The thrill of the new, the willingness to experiment and the desire to lead that animate our first supporters and set them apart is different from the more comfortable change and reliable benefits that a wider audience seeks in their quest to fit in with the mainstream. Similarly, as an offering scales, more challenging questions may be asked of its ultimate impact across society, and a greater level of responsibility may accrue.

The highest purpose of an enterprise can best be fulfilled by uniting all stakeholders in common endeavour. For stakeholder relationships to fulfil their greatest potential over the long term, they must transcend individual short-term benefits in a relationship of trust and loyalty, in which each stakeholder is not just motivated by their own material gain. During the pandemic, we saw that customers could share in and support the long-term interest of a business, with examples such as café-goers offering to bulk-buy their post-lockdown coffees in advance to help a cherished local business manage its cash flow in difficult times. A sense of purpose gives all stakeholders an intrinsic 'reason why' to join in.

Upgrade your culture

Today's culture is the product of the way things have been done before, the behaviours, habits and actions that have been rewarded in the past and the people who have best aligned themselves with that set of dynamics. It brings with it a shared way of seeing the world and tackling its problems. It guides the conversations people have within the enterprise and influences the inner narrative in each employee's mind. It is conditioned by the set of assumptions brought into being through repeated experience, which implicitly sets the boundaries on the opportunities we address as well as how we think about them and act on them.

Focusing on a Purpose Upgrade rather than simply considering options for innovation or transformation alone creates the opportunity and need to spread change across the culture of an enterprise. As Feike Sijbesma puts it, 'You need to synchronise the people inside your company and among your partners. Many people go too fast and step over why they are taking action and get too quickly to how they are going to achieve it. This leads to confrontation because people are not truly aligned.'

To upgrade your culture means to change it with intention. When you initiate new actions and recognise staff efforts differently, you create new habits that rapidly change the stories people tell themselves and each other about how things are done around here.

Culture should be specific to enterprise purpose and serve to build affinity with the business' stakeholders. If you are in the business of providing nutritious food, why not arrange quarterly retreats in which colleagues cook and eat together while learning about recent advances in healthy living and eating? Culture must be eternally renewed and benefits from the establishment of routines and rituals that both reinforce its importance and act as channels through which further learning and adaptation can be driven.

A Purpose Upgrade favours a new type of leadership across an enterprise, in which individual gain is seen as a function of competence in enabling collective benefit. It drives flexibility in the face of emergent priorities. It aligns value-creating processes with the greater capabilities of the external environment. It drives a more fluid and holistic approach to problem-solving. It replaces 'command and control' with 'seek and serve' and in so doing expands the space of achievement and increases the adaptive capacity of the business.

Upgrade your measures of success

A Purpose Upgrade can upgrade every aspect of value creation in the most fundamental way. It therefore frequently brings with it the need to change how we measure the fulfilment of our purpose.

What does each activity within the enterprise contribute to our purpose? What does each role played by members of staff contribute? What range of qualitative indicators and metrics can assess the value that is being unlocked? And how do we leave room to reward the identification and creation of alternative value that is not visible to us at the start of the process?

If we truly seek to create positive change in the world, our measures of success become interesting not just to ourselves, but to all relevant stakeholders. Would you like your customers to root for your victories and celebrate your success? What new goals can you set that mean something to everyone you need to achieve them? How will you communicate these goals? Who will hold you accountable for them? How can everyone align themselves in this pursuit?

If we are not explicit in how we define the measure of success, the default assumption among our staff and other communities will be that we are stuck chasing the same goals as any other business. This will give no one an incentive to choose us, to trust us, or to help us on our quest for better.

Upgrade your ownership

Even the ownership of the enterprise can be upgraded in repurposing an organisation. This can range from a start-up enrolling a well-known and highly regarded backer, to a global corporation intentionally seeking investors with a shared long-term vision, or even to a business seeking to bring change to the very structure of its ownership, such as by making the transition to becoming a cooperative. Rather than being the enemy of purpose, engaged investors and owners can become its most powerful enablers.

Three-question audit

The following mini audit can be applied to unlock fresh purpose for a specific activity. The questions speak to context, shared action and inclusive change.

It can be especially helpful to apply this audit to trial a Purpose Upgrade for an individual activity of importance to a business or a part of a business and to unlock learning and confidence that can subsequently support a greater Purpose Upgrade across the whole enterprise.

It can also be helpful to use this audit when an unexpected event hits the business (or indeed in the case of a society-wide crisis that hits all businesses) to identify short-term tactical responses.

1. What is needed here?

Asking what is needed takes our focus away from any single perspective and allows us to consider all dimensions of any problem or situation for all parties involved. It lifts us out of our prior assumptions and gives us permission to think from a higher ground that recognises a broader range of desires, needs and opportunities. It also serves to ground our vision in a notion of life-enhancing change.

2. How can this best be achieved?

Once we have identified what is truly needed, we can explore the best pathway for that need to be fulfilled. Again, the framing of the question lifts us out of our prior assumptions about who we are and what we do, as the best answer may greatly transcend our prior assumptions and offerings and will likely extend beyond the bounds of our own domain of action.

3. What role should we play?

Once liberated from a sole focus on ourselves and seeing the world through our own prior assumptions in exploring what is needed and how this can best be fulfilled, we can then turn to identifying what is missing: where is there a gap for us to fill that can enable the best response to the most insightfully identified need?

Hard purpose and soft purpose

We can think of purpose as having hard components that allow us to focus. They remove what is irrelevant. They set objectives, targets, milestones and metrics. And they define our most tightly controlled marketing messages. These components enable efficiency and scale.

But purpose must also have a softer side. The side that allows for peripheral vision. The side that cultivates relationships and reveals the opportunity for fresh emergence. That cultivates opportunities and allows them to grow according to their nature in ways that cannot always be foreseen.

Without hard purpose, we can't achieve efficiency, scale or coordination. But hard purpose alone leads to an inevitable decline as the shadow of what it ignores grows more and more consequential.

Without soft purpose we can't live with uncertainty, cultivate emergent possibility, or foster responsive relationships. But soft purpose alone loses momentum, can be too easily scattered and too often does not add up to enough to stand out.

Hard purpose and soft purpose combined contain the ingredients for the fullest upwards spirals of purposeful progress.

The Purpose Upgrade Credo

Our greatest opportunities are almost always out of   *.

    This is partly because they are not easy to spot; partly because we too rarely seek them out; and most limitingly of all because our repeated patterns of action and outcome determine most of what we can notice in the first place, actively preventing us from identifying the existence of greater opportunity.

    We can, however, choose to make the pursuit of greater purpose an eternal quest and make seeing through our blind spots an always-available event by asking ourselves new questions that challenge our default assumptions, awaken our perceptions to new opportunity and revitalise the actions that we undertake.

    A disposition to repurpose helps us discover greater value to create in the changing nature of our environment and the changing priorities of our stakeholders. It provokes us to find what is missing and illuminates a new path to making things better. It helps us understand and tune into the essence of the contribution we make and how we can optimise it.

    A Purpose Upgrade invites us on an adventure, calling us to fields of greater possibility. It brings forth a disposition that allows us to bring our whole selves to holistic solutions. We work more effectively and engage others more influentially because when we are always willing to adjust upwards in the light of new information, we can always fully believe in what we are doing.

    The longest journeys still begin with a single step. We can best start with micro-shifts of behaviour that snowball. We become the best version of ourselves, small action by small action, as we help others become their best selves in the same way.

    When we cultivate this approach, we build a self-accelerating

* sight.

momentum that propels us towards greater goals that we can share with the people whom we serve.

In achieving our new success, however, our new focus inevitably creates new blind spots. We must therefore renew the process, sometimes in small ways and sometimes more radically, but each time at a higher level by drawing energy and insight from what we have already accomplished.

A Purpose Upgrade takes us beyond virtuous cycles to unlock virtuous spirals of sequentially more elevated successes that adapt to a changing world.

It is never too late, or too soon to begin. But a Purpose Upgrade can always reveal what is most important right now.

Epilogue

THE ART OF FOR

Upgrading human wellbeing

After my father had one of the earliest heart transplants the local priest described him as a 'walking miracle'.

Maybe for that reason I like to train regularly to keep my heart running like clockwork. Except that it doesn't. It turns out that the true miracle of nature that is the human heart rarely beats the same way twice.[1]

The rhythm of its beat is governed by a group of 'pacemaker' cells called the sinoatrial node, whose electrical signals vary in strength and urgency so that almost every command is different. The variation in this signal balances the interplay between the sympathetic nervous system that urges the heart to beat faster and with more intensity during periods of increased activity and the parasympathetic system that works to relax it during periods of greater rest.

There is a further dynamic feedback loop between our cardiovascular and respiratory systems through a process called respiratory sinus arrhythmia that also contributes to the variation of our heartbeat through the complex interplay between these two connected systems, further accelerating and decelerating the timing of cardiac impulses to attune with the changing pattern of our breathing.

Our heartbeat not only responds to changes in our internal physical functioning but also to changes in our environment. The arrival of a sudden threat or exciting opportunity can trigger the racing of its beat to prepare us for an energetic response, just as the soothing awareness of a gentle breeze through the leaves of a forest at dusk can settle its rhythm to help us unwind.

The heart's non-linear functioning allows it to perform its mission of up-regulating our physiology in changing states of being and circumstance. As the adage that 'a change is as good as a rest' implies, this variation of the heartbeat also helps it to sustain us for the long run by reducing the overall strain on the cardiac muscles, allowing it to beat over three billion times.

Given the role of the heart in adapting to our shifts of intention from moment to moment, it is perhaps unsurprising that cardiac health is related to maintaining what psychologists call 'Purpose in Life', often abbreviated in scientific literature to 'PIL'. A study of nearly 7,000 older adults found every standard deviation increase in measured Purpose in Life reduced the risk of stroke by 22 per cent, even controlling for other biological, psychological, behavioural and sociodemographic factors.[2]

In repurposing we can draw inspiration from the human heart in powering a beating heart of enterprise, sustaining and up-regulating the systems that it depends upon and that in turn depend upon it.

A Purpose Upgrade can bring fundamental change not only to our enterprise but to our perception of the possible, to our human agency, to the paths we choose in life, to our pursuit of happiness and reward, to our relationships, to the success we work for, to our economic, social and cultural activities, to our shared futures and, ultimately, even to our own evolution as a species. It is a product of the uniqueness of human life and it can be our greatest gift to ourselves.

Upgrading economics

Conventional economics misunderstands the true nature of human experience. As we have seen, it reduces people to consumers, humans to resources and our shared home to an asset to be exploited. It isolates us from our relationships and disconnects us from our most important realities. In so doing it undermines our greatest potential.

It is unsurprising therefore that contemporary economic growth creates hidden fragilities that can undermine the very businesses that create it. Too many people would struggle to say whether the organisation that they work for is a blessing to society or a burden. Faith in our future and trust in business and capitalism has fallen to dangerous levels. What can seem like business as usual one day reveals itself the next day to have been a looming catastrophe as much for its investors as for its customers and employees.

The way out of this trap that we have now discovered is to think more inclusively and holistically and to restore the reciprocity at the heart of business, redirecting our activity with purpose-level change that we create with and through our stakeholders, revealing and bringing new possibilities into being as we go through the involvement of the very people upon whom we depend for our success. Business must be about more than the bottom line because few of the people we most need to engage to succeed care about our profits anyway. We can't just solve one part of a problem; we need to ensure that all of the parts work together in a living wholeness. My hope in writing *The Purpose Upgrade* has been to make it easier for you to lead your enterprise to success by making it a channel for something greater than itself.

Upgrading our shared future

As Mike Berners-Lee has put it to me, humankind is now in an extraordinary position. Throughout almost all our evolution, we could have done nothing to destroy the world. With the creation of nuclear weapons, we found a way to devastate at least major portions of it if we committed a grave error. Now we have reached a point where we have so much impact on the planet through our way of life that unless we change course significantly, we shall very likely bring an end to its capacity to be a liveable home for much of humankind. We have so many interconnected problems to solve, from how we feed a growing population to how we avoid further collapse of biodiversity to how we fight the emergence of new diseases. But if we are able to see ourselves as a global community and pursue a rapid path of shared purpose accordingly, there is a great deal to like about the opportunities that we can create to improve the quality of our lives while solving our most important problems. As Ian Goldin has said to me, 'Radical change, although it can seem a scary idea, is in fact a lot safer, more predictable and certain in terms of its outcomes and sustainability than continuing as we are.'

The coming years represent intertwined Gardens of Forking Paths in every direction that we can look:

- Will we live in cities, towns and neighbourhoods that are conducive to social connection and provide access to meaningful work as well as physical and mental recreation? Or will more and more of us live in conditions of isolation, exclusion and vulnerability to crime and hazard?

- Are we heading towards an automated luxury in which robotics and AI take care of our needs and liberate us for a higher order of living and working? Or a technological apocalypse in which synchronous failures leave us regularly without access to food, communications or medical support?

- Will we find a way to accommodate the climate emergency and re-configure our lives to protect ourselves and future generations while improving human welfare and restoring our relationship with nature? Or are we heading towards the mass displacement of peoples as the proportion of the earth's surface capable of supporting human life shrinks ever further?

- Will greater inclusion ensure healthy markets in healthy societies? Or will increasing inequalities mean that biofuel for the jets of the billionaires as they escape to their island bunkers prices out the availability of crops needed to feed the global peoples whose insurrections they fear?

- And will the global nature of our problems unlock new forms of international cooperation and global citizenship that secure widespread peace and mutual prosperity? Or will we regress into further conflict, isolation and a self-defeating pursuit of self-interest?

All of our choices, wittingly or unwittingly, and in some way, shape or form, take us closer to or further away from such diverse outcomes. Each fresh emergence requires us to reach new purpose and, more importantly, to empower others to do the same.

Upgrading your enterprise

We do not need responsible business as much as we need response-*able* business. A response-able enterprise actively changes the systems within which it operates for the better, integrating an understanding of their underlying dynamics and providing mechanisms that redefine how value is created in ways that create recursive benefits for all stakeholders. When such a business grows, so too do the benefits that it creates cascade across the communities that give it a reason to exist in the first place. This can enable small new ventures to break out and global organisations to break through.

To rework a thought from Aristotle: all enterprises must begin with philanthropy and all philanthropic activity must end in enterprise. If a business does not help people to secure and improve their lives and does not contribute to the society that sustains it and on which it depends, then why should it be supported? And if a charity or government department does not play some part in unlocking sustainable solutions that empower people to better help themselves and each other, how can they meet the scale of today's challenges?

A state of human flourishing combines wellbeing with challenge and brings out the best in us. When we flourish, we do our best work; we come from a place of abundance and possibility and make our greatest contribution; and the greater flourishing of the people we serve, in turn becomes the natural goal of our activity. In repurposing we can make a greater human flourishing the source, course and goal of enterprise, and in so doing unlock a greater Wealth of Change.

How will you change the world? And how will you save your business?

NOTES

Introduction

1 See *Munk Debate on Capitalism*, 4 December 2019.
2 See https://www.unglobalcompact.org for global statistics relating to the Sustainable Development Goals and their relationship to business.
3 'Ending poverty and promoting decent work are two sides of the same coin. Decent work is both the major instrument to make development happen and also in effect, the central objective of sustainable development.' Guy Ryder, Director-General, ILO.
4 United Nations World Population Projections.
5 www.unpri.org
6 See *Grow the Pie: How great companies deliver both purpose and profit*, published by Cambridge University Press in 2019.
7 See 'The Link Between Job Satisfaction and Firm Value, with Implications for Corporate Social Responsibility', published in the *Academy of Management Perspectives* in 2012. Future stock returns were chosen as a variable to demonstrate that superior working conditions were the cause rather than the consequence of the faster growth.
8 See *The State of the Debate on Purpose in Business* by the EY Beacon Institute in 2016, drawing on over 150 books and articles and complementing analysis with fresh interviews with global business leaders.
9 https://justcapital.com/reports/announcing-the-2021-rankings-of-americas-most-just-companies/

10 A Bank of America Merrill Lynch report in 2019 predicted that over the next two decades, twenty trillion dollars will flow into sustainable funds and strategies in a 'tsunami' of capital.

11 See Cone/Porter Novelli, *Purpose Study: How to build deeper bonds, amplify your message and expand the consumer base*, published in 2018, according to which 66 per cent of people will switch to an alternative product if it is produced by a purpose-driven company, rising to 91 per cent among millennials.

12 See the *Enabling the Good Life* report, published in 2017 by Sustainable Brands and Harris Poll, according to which 80 per cent of people polled were loyal to brands that help them achieve the good life, with 76 per cent saying that making a difference to others is a necessary part of the good life.

13 Research undertaken by IBM and the National Retail Federation polled nearly 19,000 people from twenty-eight countries and found that purpose-driven customers spend on average 35 per cent more per upfront cost for purchases aligned with their environmental values. See the Research Insights report, *Meet the 2020 consumers driving change*, published in the same year.

14 See Cone/Porter Novelli, *Purpose Study: How to build deeper bonds, amplify your message and expand the consumer base*, published in 2018, according to which 78 per cent of Americans are willing to tell others to buy from purpose-driven companies and 68 per cent are more willing to share content from purpose-driven brands than from traditional companies.

15 See 'Put Purpose as the Core of your Strategy', by Thomas W. Malnight, Ivy Bouche and Charles Dhanaraj, published in *Harvard Business Review* in 2019, based on an eight-year study of twenty-eight high-growth companies.

16 For example, 71 per cent of people prefer buying from brands that align to their values, rising to 83 per cent for millennials, according to the *2020 Consumer Culture Report*, published by 5W Public Relations. And Deloitte's *Retail Trends 2020* report finds that an 'authentic purpose' is now as important as digital to the next generation of customers.

17 See *The Business Case for Purpose*, sponsored by EY and published by the *Harvard Business Review*. The survey of 474 executives found that companies with a strong purpose innovate better. Fifty-three per cent of executives who said their company had a strong sense of

purpose believed they were successful with innovation compared to 19 per cent among those who had not thought about it.

18 According to the *Kantar Purpose 2020* study, brands with a high perceived positive impact grew by 175 per cent over a twelve-year period, compared to 86 per cent for a medium perceived positive impact and 70 per cent for low perceived positive impact.

19 According to the Cone Communications *Millennial Employee Engagement* study of 2016, 64 per cent won't take a job if a company doesn't have strong corporate social responsibility (CSR) values.

20 The *Deloitte Insights 2020 Global Marketing Trends Report* found that purpose-driven companies had 40 per cent higher levels of work-force retention. Benevity's Engagement Study, which analyses the activity of over two million users of its platform, also found that turnover dropped by 57 per cent in the group most engaged with their companies' giving and volunteering efforts.

21 According to the study by WeSpire, *Purpose, and the Future of Work*, Gen -Z is the first generation to prioritise purpose over salary, leaving businesses that ignore or downplay environmental impacts, have a toxic culture, or hide or spin bad news, while reading mission and values statements as a criterion to decide where to work. *Fast Company* however suggested based on a survey of 1,000 employees at large US companies in 2019 that the trend begins earlier. See their article, 'Most millennials would take a pay cut to work at an environmentally responsible company' from 14 February, 2019.

22 See *Connect: How companies succeed by engaging radically with society,* by John Browne, Robin Nuttall and Tommy Stadlen, published by W. H. Allen in 2016.

23 Stephen Warley in episode 318 of the *Life Skills that Matter* podcast.

24 According to the Edelman *Earned Brand* study, published in 2018, 64 per cent of people around the world will choose to buy or boycott a brand based solely on its stance on a social or political issue. *From me to we: The rise of the purpose-led brand*, a report by Accenture published in 2019, polled 30,000 people in a global survey and found that 64 per cent wanted companies to take a stand on current and relevant issues.

25 Published by Little, Brown Book Group, 2018.

Chapter One

1 See *Deviate: The creative power of transforming your perception*, by Beau Lotto, published by W&N in 2018.

2 See *The Knowledge Illusion: The myth of individual thought and the power of collective wisdom*, by Steven Sloman and Philip Fernbach, published by Pan in 2018.

3 See for example *From Bacteria to Bach and Back: The evolution of minds*, by Daniel Dennett, published by Penguin in 2018.

4 See for example 'Learning as an Activity of Interdependent People', by Ralph Stacey, published in *The Learning Organisation* in 2003.

5 See *Greed is Dead: Politics after individualism*, by Paul Collier and John Kay, published by Penguin in 2021.

6 See *Wired for Culture: The natural history of human cooperation*, by Mark Pagel, published by Penguin in 2013.

7 See Professor Daniel Dennett's lecture, *The Evolution of Purposes*, delivered at the University of Melbourne in 2012.

8 See *Flow: The psychology of happiness*, by Mihaly Csikszentmihalyi, Rider, 2002.

9 See the cross-sectional study by Kendall Cotton Bronk, Patrick L. Hill, Daniel K. Lapsley, Tasneem L. Talib & Holmes Finch, 'Purpose, hope, and life satisfaction in three age groups', published in The *Journal of Positive Psychology* in 2009, that showed that having an identified purpose in life was associated with the presence of hope, greater life satisfaction and higher wellbeing among the three age-groups participating: adolescents, emerging adults and adults.

10 See Pia Hedberg, Yngve Gustafson, Lena Alèx & Christine Brulin's 'Depression in relation to purpose in life among a very old population: A five-year follow-up study', published in *Aging & Mental Health* in 2010. The study of 189 people between the ages of 85 and 103 found a significant inverse relationship between a purpose in life and depression.

11 In their paper, 'The role of stress management in the relationship between purpose in life and self-rated health in teachers: A mediation analysis', published in *International Journal of Environmental Research and Public Health* in 2016, Li, Fei et al. found that individuals with more sense of purpose in life were better at managing stress and had better self-rated health status (SRH), and that stress management

partly mediated the effect of a purpose in life on SRH. The research-ers concluded that 'enhancement of teachers' purpose in life and improvement of training skills of stress management should be incor-porated in the strategy of improving teachers' health.' This recom-mendation can be applied to other professions.

12 Studies show that people with a higher purpose in life tend to engage in healthier behaviours. The study 'Prevalence of highly active adults – Behavioural Risk Factor Surveillance System', by I. Adabonyan, F. Loustalot, and J. Kruger, published in *Preventive Medicine* in 2007, found that purpose leads to greater exercise; and the study 'Purpose and health care use', by Eric S. Kim, Victor J. Strecher and Carol D. Ryff, published in *Proceedings of the National Academy of Sciences* in 2014, showed that it results in increased participation in preventive health services. This all results in better health outcomes.

13 See Nathan A. Lewis, Nicholas A. Turiano, Brennan R. Payne and Patrick L. Hill's 'Purpose in life and cognitive functioning in adult-hood', published in *Aging, Neuropsychology, and Cognition* in 2017. A survey of 3,489 adults between the ages of thirty-two and eighty-four found that a purpose in life was associated with higher scores for memory, executive functioning and overall cognition. The study by Patrick L. Hill, Grant W. Edmonds, Missy Peterson, Koen Luyckx and Judy A. Andrews, 'Purpose in life in emerging adulthood: Development and validation of a new brief measure', published in the *Journal of Positive Psychology* in 2016, also found that a purpose in life predicted better developmental outcomes, improved self-image, higher wellbeing and was negatively associated with delinquency even when controlling for personality traits among 669 young participants.

14 I have been unable to find a recording or transcript of the original version of the tale so this is a reconstruction from memory. A discus-sion of the joke, however, from *QI* series 9 episode 8, first broadcast on BBC 2, 24 October 2011, can be enjoyed here: https://www.youtube.com/watch?v=48aUMXifAn8.

15 *All Life is Problem Solving*, by Karl Popper, published by Routledge, 2001.

16 See *The Domesticated Brain*, by Bruce Hood, published by Pelican in 2014.

17 See *Enactivist Interventions: Rethinking the mind*, by Shaun Gallagher, published by Oxford University Press in 2017.

18 See *The Way Out: How to overcome toxic polarization*, by Peter T. Coleman, published by Columbia University Press in 2021.

19 The term 'affordance' was coined by the American psychologist James Gibson, best known for his cognitive theory of perception. See his paper 'The Theory of Affordances', in *The Ecological Approach to Visual Perception: Classic Edition,* published by Psychology Press and Classic Editions, Routledge, in 2014.

20 *Sapiens: A brief history of humankind* by Yuval Noah Harari, published by Vintage in 2015.

21 See *How We Are*, by Vincent Deary, published by Penguin in 2015.

22 See the works of Erik Erikson, Gordon Allport or Abraham Maslow.

23 See models of subjective well-being (SWB) such as the tripartite model by Ed Denier.

24 See Rhyff's six-factor model of psychological wellbeing.

25 See MIDUS, the Mid-life Study of Americans, www.midus.wisc.edu

26 See B. L. Fredrickson and M. F. Losada, 'Positive affect and complex dynamics of human flourishing', in *American Psychologist*, October 2005.

27 See *Antifragile: Things that gain from disorder*, by Nassim Nicholas Taleb, published by Penguin in 2013.

28 See *Happy Ever After: A radical new approach to living well*, by Paul Dolan, published by Penguin in 2020.

29 See '"How's Life?": Combining individual and national variables to explain wellbeing', by John Helliwell, in *Economic Modelling,* 2003.

30 In sociology and social psychology, an in-group is a social group to which a person psychologically identifies as being a member. By contrast, an out-group is a social group with which an individual does not identify.

31 Dreaming, for example, has been found to be a mechanism for processing anomalies in the information we've received during waking hours, helping us to establish new connections that form new patterns of understanding. See *Why We Sleep: The new science of sleep and dreams*, by Matthew Walker, published by Penguin in 2018.

32 See *The Man Who Saved The World: The astonishing true story of Stanislav Petrov*, a documentary written and directed by Peter Anthony, produced by Jakob Staberg, and released in 2014.

33 See the lecture *Human Suffering and Humanitarian Emergencies* by Professor Craig Calhoun, then director of the LSE, on 11 November 2013.

NOTES

34 See also *There's No Planet B*, by Mike Berners-Lee, revised edition published by Cambridge University Press in 2021.

35 *The Art Instinct: Beauty, pleasure and human instinct*, by Dennis Dutton, published by Oxford University Press in 2010.

36 See *Wired for Culture*, page 126.

37 See *The Best of Times The Worst of Times*, by Paul Behrens, published by The Indigo Press in 2020; also *Climate Change and the Health of Nations: Famines, fevers and the fate of populations*, by Anthony McMichael, with Alistair Woodward and Cameron Muir, published by Oxford University Press USA in 2017; and *Collapse: How societies choose to fail or survive*, by Jared Diamond, published by Penguin in 2011.

Chapter Two

1 Edelman Trust Barometer 2020.

2 See statement from António Guterres, United Nations Secretary General on 9 August 2021, upon the publication of the sixth assessment from the IPCC (Intergovernmental Panel on Climate Change): 'Today's IPCC Working Group 1 report is a code red for humanity. The alarm bells are deafening, and the evidence is irrefutable: greenhouse-gas emissions from fossil-fuel burning and deforestation are choking our planet and putting billions of people at immediate risk. Global heating is affecting every region on Earth, with many of the changes becoming irreversible.'

3 See *The Biodiversity Crisis is a Business Crisis*, by Torsten Kurth, Gerd Wübels, Adrien Portafix, Alexander Meyer zum Felde and Sophie Zielcke, published by Boston Consulting Group in 2021.

4 See *Time to Care*, a report published by Oxfam on 20 January 2020.

5 Based on data from the World Bank and Our World in Data.

6 *Enlightenment Now: The case for reason, science, humanism, and progress.* Published by Penguin in 2019.

7 *See Capital in the Twenty-First Century* by Thomas Piketty, published in English by Harvard University Press in 2017.

8 See 'The Error at the Heart of Leadership', by Harvard Business School professors Joseph L. Bower and Lynne S. Payne, published in the *Harvard Business Review* in 2017.

9 According to Gallup's *State of the Global Workplace*, only 15 per cent of employees are engaged in the workplace, only 10 per cent in Western Europe and only 8 per cent in the United Kingdom.

10 See *The DNA of Engagement: How Organizations Create and Sustain Highly Engaged Teams*, by The Engagement Institute.

11 See *Bullsh*t Jobs: The rise of pointless work and what we can do about* it, by David Graeber, published by Penguin in 2018.

12 See *The Shock Doctrine: The rise of disaster capitalism*, by Naomi Klein, published by Penguin in 2008.

13 Democratic Senators Chuck Schumer and Bernie Sanders in 'Schumer and Sanders: Limit corporate stock buybacks', *New York Times*, 3 February 2019.

14 Larry Fink's Open Letters to CEOs, 2018, 2019, 2020, 2021 and 2022. www.blackrock.com

15 Business Roundtable press release, 19 August 2019.

16 *The Economist* magazine, 24–30 August 2019.

17 Sadly, smoking is now a bigger problem than at any point in history. A study by the *Lancet* as part of the *Global Burden of Disease Study of 2019* found that the number of smokers globally had reached an all-time high of 1.1 billion, killing eight million people in that year alone.

18 See 'Young People's Voices on Climate Anxiety, Government Betrayal and Moral Injury: A global phenomenon', written by Elizabeth Marks et al, published in *The Lancet*.

19 www.refinitiv.com

20 www.ica.coop

21 According to data from KLD Research & Analytics, Inc, firms that score high on material issues and low on immaterial issues, in other words who concentrate on a few key areas, beat the market by 4.83 per cent, whereas companies that score high across the board of a materiality index perform less well. See a study of 2,396 enterprises between 1992 and 2013 called 'The Eco-efficiency Premium Puzzle', by Jeroen Derwall, Nadja Guenster, Rob Bauer and Kees Koedijk, published in 2005 in the *Financial Analysts Journal*.

22 See *The Field Guide to Understanding 'Human Error'*, by Sidney Decker, published by Routledge in 2014.

23 See *Mission Economy: A moonshot guide to changing capitalism*, by Mariana Mazzucato, published by Allen Lane in 2021.

24 Affiliated unions pay an annual fee to the Labour Party; in return, they elect thirteen of the thirty-nine members of Labour's National Executive Committee and half the delegates to the Labour Party Conference. Local union branches also affiliate to Constituency Labour Parties and their members who are also individual members

of the Party may represent the union as delegates on Labour Party structures.

25 https://www.telegraph.co.uk/politics/2022/05/07/housing-crisis-cost-us-votes-says-michael-gove/

26 https://www.independent.co.uk/news/uk/politics/boris-johnson-conservatives-rich-donors-b1898260.html

27 *Marmot Review 10 Years On*, published by The Institute of Health Equity, commissioned by the Health Foundation.

28 From the *One Barnet Transformation Programme*, 29 November 2011.

29 See *The Failure of the Free Market and Democracy: And What to Do About It*. Profile Editions, 2020.

30 *Clear Bright Future: A Radical Defence of the Human Being*, Allen Lane, 2019.

31 See *Rescue: From global crisis to a better world*, by Ian Goldin, published by Sceptre in 2021.

32 *Accountable: How we can save capitalism, stop climate change, create a fairer society and focus on purpose and profit*, published by Penguin Business, in 2021.

33 See *Understanding Brecht,* by Walter Benjamin, published by Verso in 1973.

34 The term was first introduced in the paper 'The Progress Trap: Science, humanity and the environment', by Daniel B. O'Leary in 1990. It was further popularised by Ronald Wright in his Massey Lectures of 2004 and book of the same year entitled *A Short History of Progress* and published by House of Anansi Press.

35 'Black Sky hazards' are defined by The Royal United Services Institute (RUSI) as: 'natural and man-made threats that can disrupt systems and resource-infrastructure and interdependencies upon which most of the planet depends' in an article by Director General Dr Karin von Hippel and Senior Associate Fellow Dr Randolph Kent, called 'In a world of pandemics and "black sky hazards", can the UN be rendered fit for the 21st century?'.

Chapter Three

1 See for example *The Rise of the Reluctant Innovator: When problems find people, amazing things can happen,* by Ken Banks, published by the London Publishing Partnership in 2013.

2 https://en.wikipedia.org/wiki/History_of_Google

3 https://en.wikipedia.org/wiki/Apple_Inc.

4 www.thomasedison.org

5 See *The Experience of Nature: A psychological perspective*, by Rachel and Stephen Kaplan, published by Cambridge University Press in 1989, as well as the broader subsequent field of Attention Restoration Theory.

6 See *The Wide Lens: A new strategy for innovation*, by Ron Adner, published by Penguin in 2012.

7 See *Greenovation: Urban leadership on climate change*, by Professor Joan Fitzgerald, published by Oxford University Press in 2020.

8 See 'Creating Shared Value: How to reinvent capitalism and unleash a wave of innovation and growth', re-published in *Harvard Busines Review Special Issue: How to Lead with Purpose* in 2020.

9 https://www.dailymail.co.uk/news/article-10551587/Applebees-apologizes-light-hearted-ad-aired-CNNs-coverage-Ukraine-invasion.html.

10 See also *Reimagining Capitalism: How business can save the world*, published in the UK by Penguin Random House in 2020.

11 Source: OpenSecrets.org, 23 October 2020.

12 See *Net Positive: How courageous companies thrive by giving more than they take,* by Paul Polman and Andrew Winston, published by Harvard Business Review Press in 2021.

13 See *Biophilia: The human bond with other species*, by Edward O. Wilson, revised edition published by Harvard University Press in 1990.

14 See 'Biophilia: Does visual contact with nature impact on health and wellbeing?', by Bjørn Grinde and Grete Grindal, published in the *International Journal of Environmental Research and Public Health* in August 2009, which provides a meta-analysis of over fifty empiric studies.

15 See 'The Benefit Multiplier of Investing in Nature: Solving business problems and realising multiple returns through working with ecological systems', a Business Brief written by Sissel Waage in collaboration with Restore the Earth Foundation in 2016.

16 Source: Euronews 03/04/2020.

Chapter Four

1 See *The Case Against Reality: How evolution hid the truth from our eyes*, by Donald D. Hoffman, published by Penguin in 2020.

NOTES

2 See 'Margaret MacMillan on Covid-19 as a Turning Point in History', published in the *Economist Magazine* on 9 May 2020.

3 See *Thinking, Fast and Slow*, by Daniel Kahneman, published by Farrar, Straus and Giroux in 2011.

4 See *Doom: The politics of catastrophe*, by Professor Niall Ferguson, published by Allen Lane in 2021.

5 See *Narrative Economics: How stories go viral and drive major economic events*, by Robert J. Shiller, published by Princeton University Press in 2020.

6 In anthropology this can involve the development of 'thick description' which describes not just the behaviour of humans but an explanation of that behaviour in context and in the terms of the people being observed, such that an outsider can understand their motivations, the patterns they are adopting and the stories that guide them.

7 See also Tim's fantastic book *Redirect: Changing the stories we live by*, by Timothy D. Wilson, first published in Great Britain by Allen Lane in 2011.

8 See *Happy City: Transforming our lives through urban design,* by Charles Montgomerie, published by Penguin Books in 2013.

9 See *Greenovation: Urban leadership on climate change*, by Professor Joan Fitzgerald, published by Oxford University Press USA in 2020.

10 See *The Role of Language in Emotion: Predictions from psychological constructionism*, by Kristen A. Lindquist, Jennifer K. MacCormack and Holly Shablack, published by Frontiers in Psychology in 2015.

11 Series One, Episode One.

12 www.envisioncharlotte.com

Chapter Five

1 See 'Improving Ratings: Audit in the British university system', by Marylin Strathern, published in the *European Review*, in 1997.

2 The translation is mine. The novel is called is *Les Nourritures Terrestres*, by André Gide, re-published by Gallimard in 1973.

3 See 'The Dark Side of Analyst Coverage: The case of innovation', by Jie He and Xuan Tian, published in the *Journal of Financial Economics* in 2013.

4 See *Development as Freedom*, by Amartya Sen, published by Oxford University Press, new edition, 2001.

5 See https://www.theguardian.com/business/2021/jun/10/brew-dog-staff-craft-beer-firm-letter

6 See www.worldbenchmarkingalliance.org

7 See 'Customer Satisfaction and Stock Prices: High returns, low risk', by Claes Fornell, Sunil Mithas, Forrest V. Morgeson III and M.S. Krishnan, published in the *Journal of Marketing* in 2006.

8 An annual list published by *Fortune* magazine of the 100 best companies to work for as judged by employee happiness and perks.

9 See Alex Edmans, 'The Link between Job Satisfaction and Firm Value, with Implications for Corporate Social Responsibility', published in *Academy of Management Perspectives*, 2012.

10 See 'The Eco-Efficiency Premium Puzzle', by Jeroen Derwall, Nadja Guenster, Rob Bauer and Kees Koedjik, published in *Financial Analysts Journal* in 2005.

11 www.globalreporting.org

12 www.sciencebasedtargets.org

13 www.accountablenow.org

14 www.bbc.co.uk/news/uk-england-61227709

15 https://fortune.com/2022/03/03/russia-sanctions-central-bank-ruble-us-eu-foreign-reserves/amp/.

16 See *Crashed: How a decade of financial crises changed the world*, by Adam Tooze, published by Penguin in 2019.

17 See *How to Pay for the War: An essay on the financing of war*, by John Maynard Keynes, republished by Routledge Revivals in 2020.

18 www.socialprogress.org

Chapter Six

1 See *Hit Refresh: The quest to rediscover Microsoft's soul and imagine a better future for everyone*, by Satya Nadella, published in the UK by William Collins in 2017.

2 See 'The Top 20 Business Transformations of the Last Decade', by Scott D. Anthony, Alasdair Trotter and Evan I. Schwartz, published in the *Harvard Business Review* in September 2019, and based on the study *Transformation 20* by the same authors and published by Innosight.

3 Key performance indicators.

4 Dynamically reconfigurable processor.

Chapter Seven

1 See *Value(s): Building a better world for all*, by Mark Carney, published by William Collins in 2021.
2 See *Work and Personality: An inquiry into the impact of social stratification*, by M. L. Kohn and C. Schooler, published by Ablex Pub, Norwood NJ in 1983.
3 www.zappos.com
4 www.bayer.com
5 www.tesla.com
6 www.timberland.com
7 www.ikea.com

Epilogue

1 See *Fractals: The patterns of chaos*, by John Briggs, published by Simon and Schuster Inc, New York, NY, in 1992.
2 See 'Purpose in Life and Reduced Incidence of Stroke in Older Adults: The health and retirement study', by E. Kim, J. Sun, N. Park and C. Peterson, published in the *Journal of Psychosomatic Research* in 2013.

ACKNOWLEDGEMENTS

A book begins in seed form well before the idea bursts into its author's awareness. I must therefore thank my mother and late father, Anna Mullenneaux and Nathan Skinner, for the lifetime of encouragement which gives rise to everything that I do.

I must particularly thank Anna for her unending practical support and inspiration throughout the process of working on *The Purpose Upgrade* and for working tirelessly with me to put the idea into practice.

I am also especially grateful to my editor at Little, Brown, Tom Asker, for his quiet wisdom and encouragement through-out the process of moving from idea to book, as well as to Rebecca Sheppard for her expertise in overseeing the book's production, Alison Griffiths for her copy editing and Matt Burne for the cover design.

I would like to thank Peter Cross, Dr Randolph Kent, John Marsden and Dame Fiona Woolf DBE, DStJ, DL for reading and generously sharing their thoughts on a draft of the text.

A series of conversations with Professor Mike Berners-Lee, Professor Alex Edmans, Professor Joan Fitzgerald, Lynne Franks OBE, Seth Godin, Professor Ian Goldin, John Grant, Professor Rebecca Henderson, Dr Mick Jackson, Professor Tim Jackson,

The Right Honourable Sir Oliver Letwin, Inge Massen-Biemans, Geraldine Matchett, Monique Ntumngia, Peter Seymour, Feike Sijbesma, Sir Tim Smit KBE, Daniela Barone Soares, Rory Sutherland, Caroline Taylor OBE, Dimitri de Vreeze, and Hugh Welsh were a great influence on the ideas and content of the book and provided much of the inspiration needed to complete it.

And I have learned from many others, working and collaborating with whom has profoundly shaped my perspective, including, though of course not limited to, Dr Rachelle Andrews, Dr Chris Arnold, Douglas Atkin, Khalid Aziz, Benazir Barlet-Batada, Pamella Barrotti, Mike Barry, Lisa Basford, Mandy Bobrowski, Dhruv Boruah, Raquel Buckley, Gemma Butler, Michelle Carvill, Professor Terence Cave, Rita Chadha, Catherine Cherry, Ben Cohen, Lauren Cooper, Dr Alise Cortez, Dave Crowther, Abigail Dixon, Arpita Dutt, Mindy Emsley, Mark Evans, Dr Orit Gal, Geoff Gay, Paul George, Sir Brendan Gormley KCMG, Jerry Greenfield, Robbie Hearn, Melody Hossaini, Emma Ihsan, Claire Kennedy, Christine Knudsen, Thomas Kolster, Sean Lowrie, Isabel Lydall, Ed Mayo, Gavin McAlpine, Louise McLaren, Klaus Niederländer, Lars-Peter Nissen, Professor Richard Parish, Melissa Porter, Célia Pronto, General Mark Raschke, Elaine Roberts, Professor Roy Sandbach OBE, JiaJia Smith, Debra Sobel, Sarah Speake, Laurence Stock, Kiran Sura, Dr Colin Thompson, Sue Unerman, Steve Walker, Astrid van Wanum and Stuart Wilson.

I would also like to thank every client of the Agency of the Future and each member of MarketingKind. I learn from you all every day.

Of course, none of these good people are responsible for the shortcomings of the book, which remain despite their influence and which would have been eliminated if only my desire and ability had been one and the same.

INDEX

INDEX

INDEX